SERPENT IN THE HOUSE

The Birth of Violence
In Families and Society

By D.H. Blake

AUTHOR'S DISCLAIMER

This is a work of nonfiction. Events and characters are portrayed to the best of the author's recollection. Although stories and examples in this book are true, the names and identifying details have been changed to protect the privacy of any persons involved. The ideas, opinions and words are the author's alone.

Because nonfiction is written from memory, conversations and dialogue cannot be recalled word for word with any degree of exactness. The author has taken great care to relate stories in a manner that evokes the emotions and meanings of dialogues. In some instances the author has changed characters and other identifying characteristics, such as occupations, physical appearance, locations and time for literary effect, and to assure the anonymity of individual cases. Any similarity between the characters or situations presented in this work with real people or circumstances is purely coincidental.

SERPENT IN THE HOUSE

The Birth of Violence In Families and Society

For June Elizabeth

Table of Contents

INTRODUCTION

America is under attack. Widespread acts of violence are occurring more frequently in our homes and public places than ever before. Violence undermines our personal as well as national sense of safety because its consequences affect us all. We never know when or where the next strike will be, and that is frightening. Secrecy is a powerful tool in the hands of violent people, and they take great care to hide themselves. We only find out after something bad happens.

Relationship and societal violence are the same beast in different clothing. They are flip sides of the same coin, and anger is their currency. Violence of any kind is shocking. It affects us profoundly, in more ways than we are aware of or want to admit-especially when the violence is in our own homes. Most people avoid airing their dirty laundry in public, so family conflict and abuse are usually kept private. In a broken family system, members enforce strict rules about what information is carried to the outside world. The family is untouchable. A dysfunctional family may be protected under these codes of silence for decades before secrets of violence are revealed.

Domestic violence is a monster that undermines the integrity of the family through the betrayal of trust and intimacy. Family and relationship abuse is an insidious fact of life that creates shame and rage in its victims. Its tyranny is perpetuated from generation to generation, filling hospital beds with the injured, and morgues with the dead. Relationship violence is a major contributing factor to America's societal violence. It is an integral piece of the violent culture we have become. Domestic violence is a problem grossly misunderstood by most people, and under reported by the media. It is too ugly, complicated and emotionally charged. We just don't want to deal openly with it.

Domestic violence leads to societal violence. *Serpent in the House* exposes the traits and characteristics prevalent in violent people and relationships. It clarifies the connection they have to societal violence. Violence is violence, whether domestic or societal, yet many fail to connect the two. We want social violence and domestic violence to be separate, unrelated issues. So one is sensationalized, while the other is minimized, even when it involves the horrific murders of women and children.

Violence doesn't take place in a vacuum. When humans are violent, society either acts to contain it or is part of the problem. The politics of violence are complex. Government legislates the laws by which we live, and laws set the code of conduct by which we are judged. When government abuses power, it violates the very people it is elected to protect. At some point, abused people rebel against injustice. The connection between all levels of society is significant. Like the chain reaction of cars crashing into each other on an icy road, anger at one level corrupts the others. Our culture is not re-inventing the wheel in its struggle with violence. It is the story of mankind. History is our legacy. And the past tells us what we can expect when history is repeated. We can change history in the making by changing our behavior.

There are three key points to consider as we look at domestic violence and how it expands outward to become societal violence: What characteristics does violence create in adults and children living in abusive relationships; how do individuals with those characteristics affect people outside their relationships; and, how does our culture deal with domestic and societal violence?

Domestic violence *is* social violence. Understanding how it impacts society is critical to our well-being. The issue of domestic abuse is a nasty subject that hits close to home for many people. Unfortunately, it is a reality cloaked in denial, a powerful shield with which to insulate oneself from uncomfortable truths. No one wants to be reminded of losing their temper or being in an abusive relationship. If we look in the mirror, we may not like what we see. But human beings share communal guilt for the ways we express anger in our personal and public lives. Our violent culture is telling us something about who we are. It is our responsibility to find out what that is, and do something about it.

Identifying family violence as the precursor to societal violence suggests failure on the part of public agencies to effectively deal with both problems. That concept is not welcomed. Nor is the idea attractive from a media or career perspective. It's too simple. Even sensationalizing mass killings has failed to attract the attention of major research on the connection between domestic violence and societal violence. Domestic Violence is like a cave full of poisonous snakes at the edge of town. Everyone knows it's there, but no one wants to go in and clear it out. So it's just ignored until someone gets bitten. Because nothing is done to eradicate the problem, offenses are repeated, and the perpetrators go unchallenged.

Serpent in the House takes a hard look at the conditions that enable these "snakes"- the violence-makers in our culture. It examines the threat denial poses to the quality and safety of our lives, and how we use it to protect ourselves from reality. The future of America is at stake. Avoidance of problems is not going to make them go away. History shows us that denial, and its cousin, *ignorance*, tend to unravel over time, revealing a hidden and tragic tale of woe. The intention of *Serpent in the House* is to project a bright light on the violence we face as a nation. Eliminating denial is the first step. Denial is why we have spiraled into such a moral abyss. *Serpent in the House* offers a picture of violence with the goal of awakening awareness and encouraging action.

Abuse of any kind is gross disregard for others. That includes abuses of government. With so little integrity at the highest levels of government, how can we expect our families, children, or communities to be any better? When community leaders and powerful public figures disdain responsibility, commit crimes, and violate sworn oaths, they set in motion a tone of exploitation for everyone. Exploitation is abuse. They are bullies, wielding power and arrogance against the little folk exactly like their gang-banger, hoodlum counterparts on the streets. And like their buddies in the ghettos and barrios, they seldom get caught, so the cycles of abuse continue unchallenged. Few of them are held accountable, let alone punished for their crimes.

America has drifted away from the family values and core beliefs we once held dear. *Serpent in the House* is an invitation to re-establish our integrity as individuals, families, and as a nation. The purpose is to inspire a pro-active role in the recognition, reduction, and containment of all forms of violence. Each of us have the ability to implement positive change and enjoy happier lives. Please read with an open mind. Draw on your personal resources to help prevent the domestic and societal violence that is destroying our families, schools, workplaces and country.

D.H. Blake

CHAPTER 1

Conversations With a Monster

"Swollen shut!" Mary screamed, lunging forward and grabbing the arms of the wingback. "My eyes and lips and nose were swollen shut! My face was so badly beaten I couldn't breathe!" the usual bright green of her eyes going gray as a wall of tears swept down her face. "The side of my head was gushing with blood... and I couldn't stand the pain. It blinded me... and I," she cried out, then hesitated. "That's all I can remember."

Mary angrily yanked some tissues from the box next to her, blotting the globs of mascara and mucous that had run down her chin. It had been over ten years since that escape from death at the hands of the stranger who had brutally assaulted her, leaving her to die alone at the edge of railroad tracks. And now, after spending those same ten years in prison for prostitution, drug trafficking and enduring heroin addiction, the woman who had survived so much violence was not doing well.

Her body slumped back into the cushioned chair. Lightheaded from hyperventilating through her tearful outburst, she slowly lifted her head and began breathing more easily. "Mary," I asked softly, leaning a little closer and gently placing my hand on hers, "can you tell me what happened to you that night?"

Crime scene photos, the police report and extensive medical records had documented the vicious attack, providing her with pieces of information she herself had no memory of. The assault, she had learned, should have taken her life. But somehow she had been found in time and survived; permanently disabled from the fierce blows to her head with a lead pipe, but she was *alive*.

I quietly awaited her reply. The color in Mary's face began to drain away as if she had just seen a ghost. For what seemed an eternity, a deafening silence filled the cool air between us in my dimly lit office. Suddenly, Mary was startled and jolted up out of her chair. A flashback rushed into her consciousness. The first memory since the attack had just arisen from the ashes of that brutal experience years earlier. It was intensely real, shaking her from head to toe. In a heartbeat, body and mind were remembering what had been forgotten, and it was *terrifying*.

From the darkness of memories that had become an emotional prison, Mary was being violated all over again by her assailant. What had been released from the deepest recesses of her mind was not simply the repressed memory of one attack. Like dominos in motion, an entire lifetime of trauma, violence and abuse were now awakening. Although she had been my client for months, what Mary was about to reveal would shock me to the core of my being. It would be a conversation with a monster.

BEHIND THE BLINDERS

The soul of America is in crisis, and the national pathology is *denial*. We are hunkered-down in a kind of social shell-shock that immunizes us from the frightening crimes of domestic and societal violence. There is always a method to madness. But by not looking for the madness, we won't see the method. We may think someone is acting in inappropriate or strange ways but ignore them. If something bad goes down, we'll slough it off and claim ignorance. This is *willful unknowing.* It is denial, not ignorance. "Don't want to know, so I don't allow myself to become aware; must remain oblivious lest I see something and rock the boat. What if my suspicions are wrong? I could get sued," we say to ourselves. These thoughts scare us into avoidance and silence.

Through denial, we try to protect ourselves from disturbing information and discomfort by zoning out. Denial is an attempt to control our lives by ignoring certain realties. It can also be passive, as in ignorance or absence of knowing. Dr. Martin Luther King once said that *the most serious danger to humans is ignorance.* In either case, denial lies just below the surface like a malignant tumor. Like Mary, we will not get at the underlying causes of our suffering until we open our eyes and examine the truth staring us in the face.

Because it festers, like a splinter left in a finger, denial becomes its own stressor. It is a loss of connection to the world around us and the people in it. Denial allows us to dissociate ourselves from the truth we don't want to see because it doesn't fit with the fiction we have created in our minds. Through denial we become isolated from one another in a kind of self-imposed social banishment. But humans are very social animals. As modern day members of ancient tribes, we need continuous relationship and community if we are to be happy and continue our species. Internet sites like Ancestry.com and Family Tree are wildly popular because humans seek connection to their families and origins. Social banishment is used as a form of punishment in some cultures, both human and animal. It is a state of social *dis-grace* in which few individuals will survive. But our goal as a species is to thrive, not just survive. Life depends on our ability to get along with one another, not be in constant turmoil.

Just a decade-plus into the new Millennium, America is changing dramatically. Violence, economic decline, demographic and political conflict, increasing substance abuse, and massive unemployment have led to greater stress in our lives. Every day we are bombarded by new technologies that give us amazing tools for escape from reality. It's fun, really cool stuff. Technology transports us to galaxies far beyond our imagination via chips, games and social media. But we are becoming less and less connected to each other in our quest for more.

In the 1980's, there was a T-shirt that said "he who dies with the most toys wins"! Now, over 30 years later, Americans love their toys, quick fixes and high tech devices with a passion. Sometimes that passion goes too far. For all her gifts and greatness, America has become a ravenous pop culture of chronic malcontents: ever enchanted, never satisfied. In our excesses, sober we are not. With insatiable lust for more and more, America has become the addict of the planet as well as the innovator. In our obsession for stuff we have slid into our comfort zones and gone soft. The task at hand is how to balance it all and not fall asleep at the wheel. Removing the blinders of denial will stop us from driving off into the ditch of cultural collapse.

While we were distracted, a disturbing trend took over. Political correctness has seeped into our culture. It is an attempt by a powerful movement to control much of what we think, feel, say and do. The concept of *civility* has emerged from this lobby. It is used to shame people into sameness. When free people avoid speaking up for their beliefs in fear of being singled out and punished, it is not civility. It is social engineering, and its purpose is to nullify individuality and eliminate free speech. In an era of increased bullying and violence, this kind of lop-sided, *selective tolerance* actually enables violence and crime to flourish. In effect, it is the silencing of reason. Hyper-sensitivity and the policing of speech is not civility. Enforcement of one version of good manners over the rights of others is merely a different version of power and control. It is very dangerous in a free society

With attention focused on how not to offend some people, we have become blind to the violence-creep that surrounds us. From domestic to societal violence and acts of terrorism, when the cat's away, rats play. Evil and mean-spirited people understand this. In our lockstep of politeness, decent, law-abiding people are muzzled, and criminals are getting by with murder. What we say and how we say it does not cause violence. Violent people cause violence. While what someone says may be hurtful or antagonistic, healthy people don't fire up and become violent. Dangerous people do. We are becoming a more rude and disrespectful society. It is no wonder confusion is rampant and violence thrives. Few of us know what we can and cannot say.

Emotion-based reactivity and sentimentality have replaced rational thought in answer to violence. The push to homogenize America into a populace of pre-scripted robots will not bring us peace. We have fallen victim to a more liberal standard of conduct than most of us grew up with, and it is fueling an explosion of bad behavior. In a politically correct America, crimes of violence are easily blamed on bad luck instead of bad people. We are not supposed to call someone *bad*. They are just disadvantaged by fate, upbringing or some other unfortunate circumstance. This softening of expectations is how violence continues to permeate our culture.

BLOWING SMOKE

We may attempt to adapt to this new social norm by ignoring the events and behaviors blowing smoke on our sense of right and wrong. But this kind of adaptation is not good for us over the long haul. It is *maladaptation* and will not resolve the tension and anger building up, only allow us to pretend we are handling it. Although denial seems like personal empowerment at some level of consciousness it is fake power. It is based on a lie. When we bend the truth to fit our needs, we only buy time, not strength. We are in denial.

Perpetually running ourselves on emotional and physical empty is stressful. It is an inevitable path to exhaustion. As a country divided and in conflict on so many issues, we are on that road. Stress is killing us. Just look at all the television commercials selling prescription drugs for everything from high blood pressure to sex. Dr. Sigmund Freud,[1] the Victorian psychiatrist considered to be the father of modern psychoanalytic theory, described the destructive way the buildup of stress affects us. He gave as an example a wood-burning stove with no chimney. In time, he cautioned, with enough fire, she's going to blow, and pent-up smoke will blast out sideways. America is stressed. Domestic and societal violence are the smoke blowing out the sides of our overheated, collective stoves.

In our busy lives, most of us have neither the inclination nor the energy to uphold the once deeply held values on which our families and country were founded. It's just so overwhelmingly difficult to juggle all the apples in the barrel of life. Horrible news is depressing, so it's totally natural to want to avoid it all. We don't want negative information to interfere with our main focus in life: our families, our jobs and paying the bills. But ignorance is not bliss for very long. It is a mistaken belief that if we just don't think about a problem, it isn't *really* a problem. Like termites eating through the wood beams on the ceiling: just because we don't see them doesn't mean they aren't eating us out of house and home.

Denial was not the mindset of the founders who built our nation's wealth and prosperity. Generations of families worked their fingers to the bone to give each generation a better life. America hasn't completely forgotten those sturdy roots and ethics. As more people wake up and take responsibility for the problems we face, we will see that we still have that character. It is not enough to look at the publicized events that make the headlines and rivet us with stunned disbelief or disgust. We must look far deeper than that if we are to fully understand how our society got where we are today. Our gaze will have to penetrate the truths behind the closed doors of the abusive family.

Domestic Violence is the genesis, the 'seed' of social violence. The original roots from which all violence sprouts lie deep within the recesses of family violence. Abuse stems from early life events that shaped our personalities and view of the world, and the people who cared for us. Studies of violence in relationships show how the incredibly destructive twists and turns of an abusive family or significant relationship can work to create the monster called domestic violence.

For most people, this is a very uncomfortable and rarely talked about aspect of life. But it is one everyone has some knowledge of. Relationship violence is hushed in dysfunctional families. It is minimized or reframed by media to make news that sells, and denied the public discussion it deserves. The public and media lack the willingness to get into the down and dirty of what is, for each of us, a personal connection to the violent events taking place on our watch. Our nation's societal violence is blamed on everything but the truth: the fundamental family and relationship abuse that starts it all. It is the writhing serpent we ignore. Violence is the domain of the sociopath. He cannot be denied recognition if we intend to protect ourselves.

THE BAD AND THE UGLY

Drug addictions, mental illness and personality disorders play critical roles in the molding of the sociopath. The term, Socio-path, refers to the disorder, the *pathology,* of the anti-social personality. In her revealing book, The *Sociopath Next Door,*[2] author Mary Stout presents a grim reality of the prevalence of sociopaths in our culture. It is startling, and at the same time we find ourselves nodding in agreement.

We may not know for sure that a person we live next door to, work with, or fall in love with is actually a certifiable sociopath, psychopath, or schizophrenic. However, over time we may come to strongly suspect this based on repeated unpleasant or bizarre encounters with that person. The possibility is not a comforting thought, and most people avoid such individuals if at all possible. Learning to recognize the characteristics of the sociopath is very important. It may provide us with lifesaving insight, especially when it comes to domestic and societal violence, because sociopaths commit violence.

Sociopaths, and the more dangerous version, psychopaths, are not always easy to identify. The brightest of their kind are masters of the con. They are superior manipulators, using charm, wit, talent, and often physical attractiveness to win you over. Many of these scammers are shape-shifters, able to reconfigure themselves specifically to your needs or personality as they move in on you. Many sociopaths have traits that are repugnant and kept hidden through clever and intricate facades. They are capable of carving a swath through life that is littered with the consequences of ruthlessness.

Sociopaths always have an agenda for which people are both useful, and dispensable. You may not see them pulling the wings off butterflies or beating the dog, but they cause harm, in one form or another throughout life. Many long-term studies have shown the association between animal cruelty and domestic violence. The correlation is significant. Whether attacking defenseless humans or helpless animals, the absence of compassion is predictive of the grave potential these individuals have for violence.

Communities and states around the country continue to lobby for legislation beyond the current limits of the law. It is critical that people who commit crimes against animals are prosecuted. Sadly, the wheels of bureaucracy are not yet up to speed in this monumental effort. Courts are limited in their ability to bring justice to these cases. Animal cruelty is part of the pathology of domestic and societal violence. It must be given the dignity of attention and the swift response of punishment. Successful reduction of violence requires that all forms of abuse be treated as pieces of the same package. Only the degrees of violence are different.

The monster sociopaths feed on is named power and control, and it is what grows the monster inside of them. Theirs is an existence devoid of one of the most wonderful human capacities of our species: *empathy*. Through empathy, humans are capable of compassion and caring for one another. Our empathic nature is a state of grace. It is the deepest expression of our humanity and goodness. Socio-pathy is a state of being that is *without* empathy. Sociopaths are anti-social, not social by nature. Social interaction is merely a means to their ends. Unfortunately, if empathy is not present, it never will be. Although the concept may be taught and intellectually grasped, sociopaths never get it. At the core level of their souls, true empathy and compassion do not typically exist.

Empathy is dependent on the presence of a conscience. The two interface in a symphony of humanness. Empathy, compassion, conscience, and positive regard for others are critical ingredients in a healthy human being. Sociopaths lack these qualities, or rarely show them. People who commit violence against others are either devoid of empathy altogether or have walled it off. In either case, it is not available. As a species, we pass violence from generation to generation. It may be learned, drug-induced, or mental illness related behavior, but as far as we know, there isn't a specific genetic marker for 'sociopath'. Domestic violence is not genetic either. It is learned behavior that can be unlearned. A true sociopath cannot unlearn his pathology.

Violent people can be very astute when it comes to selecting prey. They usually see themselves as the center of the universe. Most choose victims who are weak or vulnerable in order to keep it that way. Conversations with monsters are circular because they speak with forked-tongues. They manipulate confusion and chaos by twisting the reality of others and creating a closed loop. This is the domain of the serpent in the house. The goal is domination through fear. Sooner or later, victims of abuse break and surrender to their abusers. It is spiritual death; a form of brainwashing. A relationship in which a victim becomes emotionally bonded to and physically dependent on their captor is often referred to as the *Stockholm Syndrome*.[3] The threat of imminent injury or death at the hands of an abuser is a powerful force.

In the beginning of a relationship, we are usually on our best behavior. Polite and considerate, we do everything possible to win affection and acceptance from our special person. This is called the *Honeymoon Phase*. It is a time of peaceful coexistence as the parties become more familiar and comfortable with each other. It is high noon on the bright sunny hour of their relationship. In abusive relationships, the process of familiarity and intimacy is speeded up.

Moving quickly to exclusivity and commitment, the couple enmesh themselves into one entity. There are no longer two people, there is only *one* of us. This is the dynamic played out in all relationships and families that are violent. Intensity of emotion and dependence is the common denominator in the ticking bomb they are building together. The aphrodisiac of passion must be intensified in order for power and control to be established.

As boundaries of self and other disappear, the heightened sense of love is fortified. This is not the precious love between couples who cherish each other as whole individuals. Abuse-prone couples don't share the joy of building a healthy relationship based on mutual respect and inter-dependence. It is not a functional union they create together, it is dysfunctional, and will ultimately kill their love. As enmeshment tightens, the daily tick of tension and stress starts to corrode the thin veneer of attachment. Personalities and previously unimportant differences emerge and tension continues to build. And when irritations become unbearable and complaints escalate, the couple has moved to 'six o'clock'. The couple is shocked by their anger and retreats in apology and forgiveness. With renewed vows of love and the promise of never losing it again, all is forgiven. And it's back to the honeymoon once again.

The cycle with the serpent has begun. More tension, anger and attack lie just below the surface ready to launch. The pair are shrouded in hurt and distrust. At least one of these people knows exactly what is happening and where it is taking them. But they continue the dance, careening dangerously toward disaster. Each new outburst over a perceived or real insult moves them closer to the *big hurt* that lurks just around the corner. Someone is going to get it. Abusers *never* forget or forgive. Theirs is the memory of a vengeful mind that meticulously keeps score for future payback. Abusers don't care about your pain or suffering, only their own. To them, rejection is loss of power, and loss of power is unbearable. Every effort will be made to get it back.

Most people resolve conflict without resorting to abuse. Foul language, name-calling and frightening displays of emotion are not positive ways of settling differences. But in abusive relationships, the maturity required to navigate arguments respectfully is impossible. Unable to solve problems at the *issue level* of a disagreement, angry people move swiftly to the next level of intensity, the *personal attack.* At this point, combatants will hurl threats, ugly names and often whatever objects they can get their hands on in assault on the other. Once the conflict escalates beyond this point, it jumps up a notch to the *relationship level.* Potential for violence and injury is at its most dangerous peak here. The participants are out of control. They have arrived at the gates of hell. Time is up.

The original issue that started the conflict in the first place is lost in the fight. With emotions fully charged, the eruption unleashes a volcano of fury. When the firestorm subsides, the couple is moved to tears, begging for forgiveness and promising undying love in each other's arms. Exhausted, the relationship turns back the hands of time to regain the honeymoon once again. This is the Cycle of Violence, the relentless pattern of chaos that defines domestic violence. Rage is a ticking bomb, where ever it resides. As the cycle continues, the time between pressure building and explosion decreases. The once cherished honeymoon phase disappears. What remains are the narrow swings of the emotional pendulum from tension to explosion. Once embedded in this state of crises, all semblance of sanity and decency are obliterated. Without intervention, each new battle will lead to greater and more serious risk of injury or death.

In family systems, members interact to a greater or lesser degree as a social hierarchy. It may have democratic aspects, but each person in the family is not equal. Even the IRS deems one person the "head of household". Historically, that person was male. In English common law, on which our system of Law is based, males were heads of households. They held authority over all dependents and were responsible for their conduct. Specific rule validating abuse as a means of maintaining household authority has not been identified. However, legend, or possibly myth, surrounding the alleged law emerged in American women's history studies. According to the doctrine called the *Rule of Thumb*,[4] the head of household could beat his wife and dependents with a stick, provided the weapon was 'no wider than his thumb.'

The concept found its way into American life, and is cited in court cases of the late 1800's. Women were denied the vote and many other civil rights, and men may have been perceived as masters. Domestic battery was not uncommon, and women and children had minimal recourse or protection. Whether or not the rule was law or a myth, it is critical to remember that over a century later, domestic violence continues in too many households. Hitting instills fear, not love or respect. Beating anyone with anything is assault, and beating a wife is domestic violence. Both are criminal offenses. The dynamic of power in the American family has shifted dramatically in the last forty years. So has the level of stress. Relational conflict is extremely stressful and is often the reason for divorce, although it may be disguised as "irreconcilable differences". In modern society, women as well as men head households. America's divorce rate is over fifty-percent, and fewer couples are choosing to marry.

THE DISTURBED

Violent individuals can rev up their battle engines spontaneously, with little or no provocation. They dwell in an internal world unlike ordinary people. Theirs is an inferno of profound resentment and hostility easily triggered and set in motion. This is true of mass murderers, serial killers, and domestic batterers. That is why neighbors and friends often report being shocked when someone they know commits a heinous crime of violence.

The legal statutes of individual states determine the difference between social and domestic violence. The names of crimes may be the same in both categories, but the degree of relationship between the participants determines which charges are domestic. Charges are filed under *Domestic Violence* statutes when the parties involved have a relationship: by consanguinity (blood), marriage, or domicile - past or present. Whether the offense occurred at home or somewhere else is irrelevant.

Physical violence without the aspect of domestic relationship between the parties involved is assault or battery, regardless of where it takes place. If you walk into a bar and end up getting slugged, that is assault. If you walk into the same bar and slug your wife, significant other, roommate, brother or cousin, etc., that is domestic violence. Bars are notorious battlegrounds for assault. Partiers load up on liquid liberators of behavior. No news there. Substance use is commonly involved in acts of violence. People who are drinking or using, "jonesing" (craving) for their drug of choice, or hung over when things blow up are at a very high risk of violence. Danger is present when substance use is combined with an argument.

Substance use and addiction increase in times of stress across every socioeconomic group. And when jobs are scarce, money for drugs and alcohol is even scarcer. People who regularly use mood altering substances and have a low tolerance for stress and frustration find it almost impossible to stop conflict and aggression once it starts. Individuals are at highest risk of becoming violent in relationships who have low self-esteem, poor impulse control, inability to manage stress, inadequate communication skills, and broken families of origin. Pent up anger combined with low income and education levels increase that risk even more. Together, they are predictors of violence.

A history of juvenile arrests, incarceration or institutionalization also intensifies the risk for violent behavior. Other contributing factors include mental illness, disabilities, gang or other drug and violence related affiliations, and past violent episodes. Any of these factors alone, or in combination with regular or addicted use of legal, illegal, or controlled substances is capable of creating a greatly enhanced potential for violence *in anyone.*

Our bodies manufacture pharmaceuticals that are of greater purity and strength than any drug on the street. They are readily available on our inner shelf, ready to go in a heartbeat, so to say. When we are engaged in intense conflict, our angry emotions induce a rush of adrenalin and other opiate-like substances in our bodies. Chemicals meant for use in a fight for survival on the battlefield or taking on saber tooth tigers in the Stone Age suddenly crash into our brains, turning us into steroid goliaths. Called the fight-or-flight response, it is why our species is not extinct.

As the Gambler, by Kenny Rogers, says: *"you gotta know when to hold 'em, and know when to fold 'em, know when to walk away, and know when to run"*. Our bodies were never intended to live in a constant state of adrenalin-fueled anxiety. The clever stay or flee mechanism was meant to give us the option of running for our lives instead of fighting the dragon to our death. Preserving our survival hormones is important. They are a necessary buffer throughout a lifetime. Excessive stress uses them up too soon.

Angry people can become addicted to these in-body steroids as much as they would to any other drug. Adrenalin addicts are often referred to as rage-aholics. Rage addicts get off on the buzz of an elevated mood, explosive thought processes, seemingly limitless strength, and power over others. Soaring blood pressure, speeded-up heart rate, pounding temples, and the bravado of the steroid-induced fix are irresistible to an adrenalin-junkie. Others, however, like highly trained athletes, fighter pilots, officers of the law, skydivers and high wire walkers, to name a few, are also affected by internal steroids.

Participating in sports or performing on the job duties is an entirely different use of these drugs. The classic "runner's high" is a well-known and enjoyed state experienced by joggers everywhere. It's not the same as pumping a load of bullets through a locked door after an argument with a girlfriend while listening to her screaming as she's hit, like the "Blade Runner" in South Africa.

For angry people, the rush is part of the rampage, maybe even a goal. But coming down after a violent episode can bring on a harsh hangover. Detoxing from such a strong drug renders an unwelcomed emptiness and a bleak depression in a body depleted of its chemical soul mate. Before long, the addict will need another dose to pacify the beast within and start the whole process over again. This is one aspect of domestic violence that is so difficult to treat clinically. Even individuals who have no history of substance use may be profoundly addicted to the drug of rage. It is that strong, and very hard to kick.

If we don't recognize destructive and violent tendencies in people, we can't take steps to protect ourselves. We might unsuspectingly be having a conversation with a monster over lunch. Behind a pleasant face may be a person we don't really know. Recognizing behaviors and reading body language requires a critical skill: *discernment*, the ability to tell the difference between smart and stupid, good and bad, right and wrong, sane or insane. Discernment is the thought process that might save our lives by keeping us out of relationships with troubled people, no matter how charming they might be. Mood-altering substances make it difficult to exercise discernment and cloud other decision-making processes. For that reason, sociopaths may frequent bars and other party venues looking for their next quarry.

Not all sociopaths are violent. Some of the brightest stars in certain professions and businesses exhibit the characteristics found in sociopaths. According to Dutton,[5] in his research on the careers and jobs that are most attractive to the classic sociopath, we can expect to be surprised at the success and prestige that is garnered by this lot. Excellence and achievement in the sciences, research, business, technology and medicine are among the many examples of the benefits we have gained from these highly talented and productive people. Violent people are a special breed of sociopath. Care needs to be taken in correctly identifying them.

THE LITTLE BALLERINA

It is important that we look at both sides of the sociopath to see what, if anything we can learn for the betterment of us all. One side is extremely dangerous to society, and the other can be exceptionally constructive to our common good. Careful discernment, intuition, and paying attention are essential to helping us recognize non-violent as well as violent people.

Let's consider in more depth exactly what the relationship is between us and our fellow loner, anti-social, violent, damaged and pathological humans. We do have a relationship, a binding social contract, whether we admit it or not, with all others in our culture. It is crucial that we accept and understand this fact. Realizing our social context with each other will help us find a way through the perilous straits of violence and terrorism that we are confronted with in contemporary America. To that end, let us look at the case of Angela.

Petite, and dedicated from early childhood to her love of the dance, Angela, we will call her, had developed into a talented ballerina by age sixteen. She had also developed into a party animal. Peer pressure, anorexia and smoking so common among dancers trying to stay tiny, and the strenuous physical demands of ballet caused Angela chronic, severe *pain*. Struggling with school, substance abuse, drug-using friends and her broken family, she also experienced constant emotional and physical stress. "It is too hard to deal with it all!" she had insisted, rationalizing the heavy use of prescription drugs she was stealing from her mother or buying on the street.

"My mom and dad hate each other, and he's so strung out now since the divorce, he's useless. I hate him. He's a junkie, that's all. He beat me and he beat my mom and he's a loser. He can go to Hell! Moms' just as bad. She just hides it better. It's her fault he beat us." Angie added another resentment: "And she steals drugs from the hospital...when patients die or are discharged. Instead of following the rules and throwing them away, she brings them home. That's how she stays baked all the time. And, that's how I get my stuff! She's so freakin' out of it. She doesn't even know how much is in the kitchen cabinet. I take whatever I want, whenever I want. My mother is clueless. I hate her too."

Angie, as she liked to be called, was a bitter teenager caught in a horrible trap of abuse and unhappiness. It was a revolving door of family violence that went as far back as her great grandparents. "People beating their wives and girlfriends and doing drugs is a way of life for my whole family," Angie snarled, when I suggested she could be the one to break that cycle, if she wanted to. What she wanted was to be liked and loved.

Angie lived with constant pain in her feet and legs, and hated her family. Her only comfort was with friends, and an addiction to narcotics that consumed her. All she wanted was a better life. What she got was a second chance. When a bad drug trip got her busted by none other than her mother, Angie was hauled away kicking and screaming to an inpatient treatment program. Detox was harsh. She hated the sudden dawn of reality, and deeply mourned the loss of her narcotic crutches. But she completed the program, and came home a new kid! She found a part-time job, went back to school, and planned to go to college. Ballet returned as the love of her life.

Angie stayed straight for a year. And then, she went missing one night after closing the fast-food store downtown where she worked. When she missed our appointment the next day, I called to see if she was at her father's house. "Maybe she just decided to stay over at a friend's instead of going home late to her mother's," he said calmly. Angie and her dad had both gotten clean. Neither of them were drinking or using drugs. They were seeing me weekly for family therapy and had reconciled with each other. It was going well. Angie loved her new and sober life, and Carl was happy for the first time in decades.

He slapped her around a lot when she was little, he admitted. Carl and Angie's mother argued constantly, especially when they drank and got high. He was a raging bull when he was mad. And Angie's younger brother ran away and hid when the fighting started, leaving Angie to try and protect their mother. "Angela was sweet," Carl said. "But sometimes she just got in the way. I never meant to hurt her. She just looked too much like her mom. I couldn't help it!" he continued.

"All I ever knew was how to be a macho man. A real man ruled his home. That was what my dad did, and his dad, and it was supposed to be me too." Carl continued. "Angie was a little flower, but I beat her, and beat her mother in front of her. I hated myself afterward, but

I didn't stop." His face contorted with the self-loathing that comes from hard core honesty in early recovery.

Carl admitted he was crazy when he used drugs, and nasty when he didn't. He was just plain nasty. Mean, vicious, and nasty. "As much as I hated my own father for what he did do me, my mother and my brother, and swore I'd never be like him, I became him." Carl's voice went hoarse. He was alone in my office, a broken, deteriorated, pitiful man. The little ballerina had never come home. She had never gone to a friend's house that night after work. A year had passed, and the police had no case. It was cold. The family was destroyed by the anguish and unknowing. But one day Angie's mother called my office. She was distraught and sounded heavily sedated.

"It's me, Katherine." She sobbed uncontrollably, impossible to understand. Angela's step-father took the phone. "Hello, Donna, I'm sorry……..but - we have some news. *It's Angie,"* he whispered. After a long silence, he continued, "they found…..ah, the police - they found…" the man struggled to speak, nearly gaging as he formed the horrible words: "a pair of feet have been found…in an old dumpster …downtown! "

"Feet?" I asked faintly, in utterly stunned disbelief.

"Feet. Just feet. They think it is, they…..are….Angie's." the man sobbed, and I heard such piteous crying in the background. It sent shockwaves through my body. "Katherine will have to go down to make an identification." My heart pounded with horror. If it was Angie, there was a vile, dark feeling that there might be some kind of symbolic meaning to such a mutilation. Her feet severed? Where was the rest of the ballerina? *Who could do such a thing?* All I wanted to do was vomit.

Angie had brightly painted toenails and wore thin, gold-braided rings on the second toes of each foot. Her feet were her craft, and she took care of them. Despite the painful bunions and blisters that adorned the deformed but muscular toes, they were her pride and joy. If the feet found in the dumpster were hers, there would be no mistaking them. And in the end, they were indeed Angie's decomposed, unique limbs. The small gold rings were there. Her feet were all the family would recover of their precious daughter. So they placed them in the earth and said good-bye. Not at rest, not in peace or hope, only in profound grief.

For Angela, the family violence had stopped when her parents divorced, but in reality, violence in her life was just beginning. As a child, a deep, searing wound had been opened in her little spirit. The die had been cast, just like it had been for Carl, her father, and her drug addicted mother.

CARRYING THE TORCH

Generations of familial violence, drug abuse, and stress had left their mark on Angie. The mark of the serpent was on her back. She was delicate, vulnerable, struggling to get it right in her life, but predators can smell their prey. And once he set his sights, the monster hunted her down like a cobra.

The night Mary was brought into an emergency room nearly bludgeoned to death, she was selling her body on the street. A prostitute, an addict, she was also marked by the monster of family violence. Following the path of crime and violence she knew so well from her brothers, father, and mother, bright, beautiful Mary lost her way. And almost her life. The same man who hacked the tiny dancer to pieces also left Mary for dead. On separate nights, in one city, he destroyed two very different yet similar human beings. One in death, and one in life.

Years later, the killer was finally apprehended because Mary had survived his rampage. Once she remembered everything that had happened just before her beating, she was able to help law enforcement find the killer. As a result of her effort to heal and the years she spent in recovery, she was able to describe in detail his appearance, voice, eyes, and behavior. Before attempting to kill her, the murderer told Mary about the '*other girl he did*'...and described how he was going to do it to her as well. But he was careless, and Mary put up a loud and desperate fight. Ironically, her own history and experience with violence saved her life.

SOME DIE SO THAT OTHERS MAY LIVE, is a sad and accepted truth in recovery from addiction. Angela will never dance *Swan Lake* with the New York City Ballet. But before she died, she was able to break the lifetime cycle of violence she was a victim of. Her lesson is for all of us: *We can't change others, but with commitment and a willingness to open our eyes, we can change ourselves.* Although his heart was broken, Angela's father picked up the torch. He shared the message of his daughter's story everywhere he went. Carl wanted people to find life through the tragedy of her death. There is no erasing the past or removing the vulnerability others have deposited in our souls. But we can create a new reality.

When the killer's life story was disclosed, it was sad but not surprising to learn how closely the sadistic killer was linked to his victims by similar childhood experiences. Shared histories of violence, substance abuse and anger rendered victim and killer unconsciously attractive to one another. Angela's assassin was twenty-nine when he took her life. Big blue eyes and thick sandy hair accentuated his boyish good looks, and his name suited him well. Conley, I'll call him, worked as a day laborer, and females were drawn to his sensual physique and polite manner wherever he went.

When Conley was eleven, his twenty-five year old mother died from a botched abortion. She was a prostitute, and his father was one of her customers. But the boy never knew who he was. His mom was beaten and drugged most of the time, and her pimp hated him. He tried to kill both of them one night in a drunken rage. The child's life was a nightmare. By the time he was old enough to understand it all, Conley awakened to the monster inside of him. Filled with hate and rage, the boy swore to make hell the focus of his life. His first sexual experience with a girl was his first murder. She was seventeen; Conley was fourteen. The crime initiated his life as a serial murderer. And it sealed his place in purgatory.

Mary went on with her life. She maintains sobriety one day at a time, and was graduated from college with a degree in education. As a teacher, Mary shares her life experience as an inspiration to others. She teaches about life and studies life to be a mentor to others. Her life is a model for what the human spirit is capable of achieving.

What you can do: If you are in a violent relationship, get out! Seek help and shelter immediately. If you are in an abusive relationship, job, or circumstance, consider counseling and support groups. Examine your own anger, and commit to learning skills for managing stress and conflict. Encourage others in your life to do the same.

CHAPTER 2

THE SOCIAL CONTRACT

Fireworks hissed as they shot into the dark sky from the yard behind Martin's house. Explosives were illegal, and it was two in the morning, but the police didn't show up. They were probably not even called. It wasn't likely they would come if they had been. Some things were just left alone in Barrio Viejo.

This was not a party anyone wanted to complain about. Everyone in the hood understood that. The *homies* celebrating at this fiesta were *Crips*. And lots of them. In fact, the family occupying the party house consisted of several generations of bangers so deeply imbedded in gang lifestyle that their combined rap sheets were thicker than a stack of dictionaries.

With rockets soaring and crackers popping, the rest of the historic barrio lay awake. Worried families huddled in their beds, anxiously waiting for the bullets to start flying. As the pyrotechnics got louder, the crowd got bigger. Boom boxes blasted vulgarities into the crisp night air as partiers yelled and screamed over each other. Cars peeled recklessly in and out, leaving rubber and beer bottles on the street behind. The party turned into a drunken orgy. Martin and his friends decided to leave his vacant property and head home. They knew it was time to get out of there, but he wanted to do one final walk around to be sure everything was locked and secure.

"The house was a foreclosure, so I bought if for peanuts. It was a "flipper," a rehab project I finished and was ready to put up for sale." Martin recalled, two months after that life-changing night. "Since it was in a high crime area, I worried about vandalism and tagging. I was checking on it every day. The final clean-up was done and I moved my tools and stuff out," he continued, his face pale and inanimate.

Martin learned carpentry, plumbing and just about every skill he needed to remodel houses from his father. He intended to make a lot of money on the side rehabbing in the city's booming real estate market. Young, single and physically strong, he knew he had about five or six years of buying and selling fixer-uppers ahead of him. His goal was to make a fortune before quitting his day job. With a nice, passive income from rentals and flips, he would be financially set by age thirty. He dreamed of having a wife and family one day. Martin wanted to show off the house to his girlfriend and friends. It took him six months, eighteen hours a day working two jobs, seven days a week. He had a good eye for detail, and felt a lot of pride in his work. It was time to move on to the next one.

"We were all out for dinner and made a few club stops to meet up with some other people. Afterward, we went by the house to have a beer before calling it a night." He was not at all shaken as he told me what had happened. "None of us were drunk, just 'buzzed', but I was really tired," he added. "I'd had problems before with the people behind me. I should have known better than to show up at the house with all of them wasted back there. The one brother, a real loser, threatened me a couple of times, and I was ready if he tried anything stupid on me."

"What does that mean," I asked, "*ready?*"

"He was a punk - a wannabe gangster. When I was working on the house he always flashed his knife or piece at me from the wall between our yards. If he wanted trouble, I was ready. I had a permit to carry, so I was always armed when I was down there working on the house." Martin flashed a vacant glance at me, expecting a reaction to the mention of a gun. But my daddy was a Kentuckian who taught me how to shoot when I was very young. It didn't faze me. He had a right to bear arms. What concerned me was the coldness in his eyes and voice. Something terrible had happened that night, and here we sat, having a calm, cool conversation about it.

Martin took a slow, deep breath and moved his eyes away from mine. "Julio was his name. The little punk *Crip*. Kept sticking his head over the wall to yell at me about how he was gonna make his bones in the gang by offing me in my yard. I doubted he had the cajones to do that, but he was a speed freak and a drunk. Anything was possible from the jerk," he added, shaking his head. "I was sick of his mouth. If he ever came at me I was going to take him out first. All I really wanted to do was finish the house and get the heck out of there. I guess that wasn't gonna be the case." He pursed his lips tightly and looked blankly into my eyes. "Julio called the shots on this one."

Martin was a hunter. I knew this from the time I first met him in his early teens, along with his brother and his father. I had a pretty good glimpse of what their lives and home were like. The three of them lived together like mountain men on the small ranch Martin's father owned. They were self-sufficient, self-contained men who went heavy on the *sauce*. Most of what they consumed was home-brewed or distilled in the old barn on the back acre of the property. Raising livestock and chickens for slaughter and a garden full of vegetables kept the three of them well fed and busy. But father and sons were high on one substance or another most of the time Even so, school was attended, sports played, and jobs held down. The family was functional to the teeth, despite the drugs, alcohol and underlying drama of domestic violence that punctuated the household.

Martin wanted to live. He also wanted to take charge of the situation he found himself in instead of avoiding it. "When I went out to the back yard, Julio saw me and starting yelling obscenities at me. He was waving a wicked-looking blade over his head, and started hoisting himself up onto the wall. I took only a couple of steps into my yard, but the wall was less than five feet high, and his shoulders were already up on top."

"What was he yelling, Martin?"

"He said: 'You're a dead man now. You're done!' I told him to shut up and get off my wall, but he kept coming over. He was babbling, really drunk."

"What were you thinking at that point?" I asked.

"I can't let him get over the wall."

"So what did you do then?"

"I went back inside and told the others to clear out, to go out the front door fast. Then I got my gun and went out to the yard again." Martin stopped talking, casually rolling his thumbs around each other as he raised his eyebrows and stared unemotionally at me. "He just kept coming; his arms, and then his leg came over the wall. I told him to stop."

"Did he see the gun?" I wondered out loud. "Did Julio have a gun too, Martin?"

"I don't know." Martin paused a moment, then finished. "In a few seconds he straddled the wall ready to jump. He was nuts, yelling over and over he was going to kill me." I didn't want to hear what came next. The look on my client's face was icy and intense.

"What then, Martin?"

"So I shot him! Dropped him cold. One shot-in the head."

At this point, there was no movement in Martin's face, only an eerie calm. Rather than making the choice to lock up and exit the property with his friends, Martin made a fatal decision. One that cost a kid his life. A momentary act that gave him a permanent felony and seven years in prison. All he had to do was leave, but everything the man was and everything he knew told him to stay and solve the problem his way.

Julio did not have a gun. The party had indeed been a bad scene with lots of dangerous people. That was undeniable. Now, most of the dead teen's family, friends and gang members would be looking for Martin for the rest of his life. Martin bought into the mistaken belief that violence was the way to resolve the problem with Julio. An abusive childhood, substance abuse, and his short-fused temper had converged in one irreversible act: the killing of another. Julio was an equally damaged and angry guy, but that won't matter to his gang family. Martin was now a dead man walking. He had a contract on his head.

In the 1950's, penal and mental health institutions were antiquated facilities reflecting the beliefs and attitudes of America at the time. They were barbaric systems in desperate need of reform. So when a new generation of criminal offenders descended on those systems during the Viet Nam Era, there was chaos. Prisons, mental hospitals, and the Veteran's Administration were taxed beyond their capacities. Psychiatric institutions closed their doors as mental health laws changed, releasing thousands of patients back into society. Bigger prisons were built to address the flood of convicts entering the system. Suddenly, criminals, the mentally ill, and drug addicts found themselves thrown together behind bars. As a result, prison populations grew fat with a culture more dangerous than ever before. Martin was housed in one of the roughest of those prisons to serve out his sentence.

AGREEMENTS WE MAKE

By definition, violence is the physical, mental, human and natural *infliction of harm and damage by force or power*. It is without mercy, leaving human beings ravaged, and property decimated. When acts of brutality are of human origin, they are more psychologically traumatizing than the havoc Mother Nature causes. Nature acts indiscriminately, not personally, and we get that. It is when the intention to cause harm to another is calculated that it causes such profound suffering. Human cruelty is difficult to understand, but its existence must not be denied.

To understand how we as a culture may be aiding and abetting violence, we must first recognize it in our own lives. Listening to news about bad things happening in our communities, like our parents and grandparents did, isn't enough. Our country has changed. We live in a much more dangerous world. Violent crimes are everywhere. They are in our homes, not just out there somewhere else. People have to be informed about violent crime on a much deeper level. If we are going to make our homes, neighborhoods, and country safer, we will have to see all human acts of violence as personal.

But people take action only if physically or emotionally compelled to do so. Many of us are too busy to get excited about another murder or vile crime in the news. Too much information heaped on us when we are already overwhelmed leads to emotional absenteeism. We just tune it out. Apathy has become a significant trait in the cultural psyche of America. It is a troubling state of mind for a once great society. Violence is trickle-down misery we are all victimized by. It affects us in one way or another, sooner or later.

To deny our own roles in the violence that has corrupted our country is a cop out. Like selective hearing, it is dishonest. We are a nation of over 300 million people bound together by social contracts. Every day we make agreements with ourselves and each other. They define our integrity and pathos as human beings as well as a nation. Agreements establish the norms and values that reflect our beliefs. But looking at violence in America, it is hard to imagine very many of us wanted to be where we are: on a very slippery slope. Many feel a sense of hopelessness as we watch America slipping further into anger and conflict. We seem to be in a downward spiral of unhappiness. But there is no one to blame but ourselves for the meanness we experience today. It is the natural consequence of failing social values, the breakdown of the family, and denial.

America is losing the ancient compass of morality she was founded on. It is the same compass which still guides all moral people around the world, but it is rarely taught in our schools or families today. Principles, morals and decency are irrelevant in a pop culture where it's not cool to be limited by a conscience. Morality is equated with religion by those devoted to the pursuit of self-gratification. And to the devoutly liberated, religion and spirituality are an infringement on that pursuit.

Across the planet, millions of people of great moral direction choose to live lives of virtue. Universal morality is non-denominational, it is, rather, a sign of character. In the blossoming of the 'new world order' in America, the pursuit of virtue is an extinct dinosaur. The concept of "character" has become Tyrannosaurus Rex, and the difference between right and wrong is optional. Like Faust,[1] we are making a pact with the devil, and it is changing the quality of American life and liberty as we once knew it. With that pact, we are enabling the expansion of the very acts of immorality, crime, and violence that are making us unhappy, disillusioned, angry and scared.

SHATTERED DREAMS

The problem with moral people is just that: they are moral. It is not typically in their blood to act viciously or react aggressively unless it is a matter of life or death. Even then, the will to live is not the same in all of us, moral or not. Some people embrace such an absolute philosophy of passivity that even the instinct to survive will not trump the position. Participation in any act of violence or aggression, even to stay alive or protect another, is unconscionable. Others, like Martin and Julio, have no qualms about using violence. Such differences in human nature make social agreements subject to interpretation. From the criminal to the pacifist, and the vast range in between, human beings don't agree on much.

Two tragedies took place decades and continents apart. They illustrate the degree of variation in how people view life and themselves in it. The first was memorialized in the movie, *Alive*.[2] It was based on the true story of a team of athletes on a fateful flight that crashed into the Andes. Most of the players, their friends, accompanying family members, and crew were killed on impact. There were few survivors. The shattered fuselage became a garish morgue of warm, dead bodies as it lay torqued into the snow and ice of the mountains. A scene of unimaginable horror faced survivors. Those who were able rallied to the desperate situation, finding and caring for wounded as best they could. Securing food, clothing and shelter became increasingly difficult in the freezing, thin air that enveloped them. Long, bitter days in the aftermath took their toll. The injured continued to die. Those remaining ran out of food.

Survival looked grim. They desperately needed to eat. A painful decision was made. The men would have to commit the unspeakable act: *cannibalism.* They would eat the dead scattered around them. Some of those who said yes, lived. Others for whom the option was intolerable, perished. The decisive factor was the will to live. It enabled the men to keep going, for themselves and for each other. Some view the willingness to eat human flesh as a ghastly, horrific, even evil act. Others admit they would make the same choice if it meant staying alive. Ultimately, courage and will brought the remaining members of the team home. That is what we are capable of. In the tragic irony of the accident, some dreams were shattered – others, fulfilled.

The next incident reveals a completely opposite human response to death, dying and humanity. It demonstrates a different kind of social contract. An elderly female resident suddenly collapsed in the dining room of an independent living facility in California.[3] Independent means residents are capable of living with little or no assistance. As she lay on the floor gasping for air and unable to breath, we listen to the 911 call made by a nurse-employee at the side of the fallen resident. When told by emergency services to immediately begin CPR, the employee calmly and matter-of-factly declines that instruction.

The dispatcher pleaded in disbelief, begging the nurse to hand the phone over to "anyone", even a passerby, to help. She asked her "as a human," to get anyone who could begin the emergency procedure on the dying woman. They needed to keep her alive until EMS arrived. The employee again refused. This went on for more than five minutes. She would not hand-off the phone or make any effort whatsoever to get someone else to assist the victim. The *nurse* quietly repeated that the protocol and policy of the facility did not allow employees to administer medical services.

The protocol and policy? Allegedly, the elderly woman had not previously signed a DNR (*Do Not Resuscitate)*, the medical directive to deny drastic emergency resuscitation in the event of death. The facility and employees wouldn't even ask someone who was not an employee for help. The woman died. In a public statement released by the family, a daughter who was reportedly also a nurse, allegedly supported the decision not to give emergency CPR. The family apparently agreed it was OK to let her die. Different people have differing views on the value of life. But we would hope that someone would help us in an emergency instead of just letting us die. Especially in a facility with medical staff trained to do so.

Is this behavior negligence, or merely an example of the range of human capacity for compassion? Either way, it is choice. Quite simply, in this case, many people were in a position to determine whether another lived or died. In nature, survival of the fittest weeds out weaker, less fit individuals, allowing for only the strongest to thrive and procreate. But sometimes survivors needs help. We see in these two stories the best we are, and the worst. A few men stranded on a mountain demonstrated superior fitness for life. With determination and compassion for one another, they chose to risk everything in order to live. The other exemplifies a very dark act of cruelty and immorality. Those of us with grandmothers, mothers, daughters, sisters, friends or wives can only imagine what we would have done in this case.

The Good Samaritan Act is a law in most states that provides legal protection to people who give emergency aid, regardless of the outcome. It is one of the most important social contracts we have. Some people are born with the instinct to survive and the compassion to help others. But not all. Can we expect to see outrage over this act of inhumanity? Not likely. It was a passive act of violence, but like too many others, the incident will simply fade away. It is part of an emerging trend in our culture that devalues the very young and the very old. In this incident a woman's life was less important than a person's job. Corporate policies and procedures determined the outcome, not sympathy or compassion.

In each story we see firsthand the depth and diversity of the social contract by which we all live or die. Many countries in the world revere the elderly. Not here. In a country obsessed with youth and the façade of youthfulness, America desperately fears and dislikes old age. Domestic abuse and violence against the elderly is a pervasive crime in America. Elder Abuse is on the increase because millions of aging people are living longer than previous generations. Older adults are dependent on the care of others, sometimes for decades. The potential for abuse is huge, as senior citizens lose independence, health, and their homes. A country without charity and kindness for its populace is a country in trouble. Tolerance of abuse and acts of violence negates our humanity and enables further victimization.

Strangers, family members and caregivers are common abusers of the aged. Nursing homes and other assisted care facilities are also sources of the phenomenon. Elder abuse is criminal behavior. But it is difficult to expose in an aged population of helpless, frail, and disabled adults. Especially vulnerable are victims of Alzheimer's and other memory loss diseases. Because it is usually done without witnesses, geriatric abuse is even harder to prosecute The oldest, like the unborn and those unfortunate enough to be born viable but unwanted, are becoming *throw-a-ways* in our culture. Maybe it isn't the contract we thought we were agreeing to when we forgot to pay attention and got swept up in our changing culture. But it is the contract we have.

Baby Boomers are the largest generation in America's history. They are also the next geriatric citizens who will need assisted living and long-term care. Ironically, Boomers have reached the ages of the parents and grandparents they once rebelled against; a day they never imagined when life was young and carefree. Now, steaming ahead and beyond the century mark, Boomers spend billions of dollars on vitamins, plastic surgery, Botox and hormones. Millions of youth-seekers try frantically to turn back the hands of time. But the resulting illusion of youth is phony and temporary. Despite the miracles of medicine and chemistry, Boomers are greying, wrinkling and sagging. So too is the nation's culture Boomers helped create.

Over time, a privileged generation changed the values of America to meet its needs. Now we need to get those values back to change America.

IT'S COMPLICATED

In the past fifty years, justice has tilted toward a softer, gentler way of dealing with criminals. Underscoring this shift is a belief that anyone can be rehabilitated. No matter what crimes someone may have committed, with proper therapy and a second chance, criminals are capable of positive change: becoming good, productive citizens. Courts, laws, the mental health industry, and many prisons reflect this trend. The theory is well-connected and funded. Because attitudes have shifted to the side of the perpetrator in some instances, mercy is more often extended to the criminal than to victims in the courts today.

It's becoming more common for victims to be cited by juries and aggressive legal teams as instigators or guilty parties in crimes. This is how rape victims were treated before *Rape Shield Laws*[4] were established to protect victims of rape. Misguided intellect and empathy perpetuate this kind of insanity. In the politically charged world of social justice, facts about the criminal and the criminal mind he possesses are often ignored. Criminal behaviors are explained by a rotten childhood, addiction, mental illness, or just plain, old bad luck. A 2014 report by the National Substance Abuse and Mental Health Services Administration (SAMHSA) estimates that 4% of the population are "seriously mentally ill" (SMI).[5] That means about twelve million people have severe mental illness. They aren't all criminals. Myriad technicalities in the law are often invoked to free accused individuals. In such cases, the technicality becomes justice, not truth.

Statistics do not validate leniency as a positive approach in corrections. The odds for remission of criminal thinking and behavior in offenders are not good. In reality, very few felons are habilitated. Rare are the individuals in warm and fuzzy programs who truly change their ways. Instead, we see higher rates of recidivism (re-incarceration) not lower. Repeat offenders are the norm, not the exception. That is why prisons are overcrowded. Private prisons are big business in America. Investment opportunities grow with the increase in crime and the recidivist population. The Criminal Justice System isn't working very well because we as a society aren't working very well. We have enabled our problems by raising our tolerance level and lowering our standards.

In reality, mostly *hardened criminals* emerge from the mean yards of America's penitentiaries, not *pussycats*. Denial of the profoundly embedded essence of criminality that exists in most criminals is negligence. It condemns society to perpetual acts of violence. When prisoners are released, a social contract is made: one by the parole board and mental health providers, the other by the parolee. If we are guided by leniency instead of caution, parole will initiate the cycle of crime all over again.

Prison systems and inmate populations provide their own social contracts. Convicts quickly learn that obedience and conformity to those contracts means food, power, protection, and survival. Non-compliance means abuse, violence, solitary confinement, hospitalization or death. Harsh lessons become a way of life. A common joke amongst inmates and ex-cons is how they learned more about crime inside than they knew outside. They are re-habilitated by pros on the inside of the bars, not the therapy team on the outside. Rehabilitation in this case is not good. It is not learning how to live straight, law-abiding lives. What ex-cons take back to the outside world is a reframed and improved criminal lifestyle.

PRETTY IN PINK

Recidivism is rampant for hard-core criminals. It's really hard to behave outside of prison once there's no guard or punk in your face to answer to. Some ex-cons earn power and easy money when they get back in the hood-until they start making mistakes. Sometimes it's their big mouth. For others, it's a small brain that gets them into trouble. It's usually both. But criminals back out on the street are always just one step ahead of the law. It is simply who they are and what they do. Offenders offend. The classic irony of the repeat offender is the alternative option to a life of crime in society. Some felons find it easier to opt back into the system than trying to stay legal on the outside. The security of three hot meals, a dry warm bed, and clean clothes every day looks better than homelessness. It is the re-incarceration-by-getting-busted trick.

Many criminals who have spent more of their lives institutionalized than free don't know how to make it on their own. For them, going back in is going *home*. This option is not as tantalizing to detainees sent to Sheriff Joe Arpaio's "Tent City" near Phoenix, Arizona, however. Tents provide no air-conditioning, special meals, or the accoutrements found in some high-end country club prisons around the country. Inmates clean up highways in chain gangs, endure harsh extremes of weather, live in large tent-barracks, and eat peanut butter and baloney sandwiches. They get zero special treatment from guards, and: *they wear pink underwear.*

Activists protest that conditions in the camp are inhumane and un-American. But it works. The "Sher", as he is called, runs a highly successful program for the criminally penitent in the Arizona desert. "Once is enough," I have been told by many who have served time in the tents. Perhaps, as the Sheriff suggests, they go somewhere other than Maricopa County to commit crime these days. Because Tent City means hard labor and bare-bones housing, it is a very effective deterrent to crime. The facility boasts a significant reduction in recidivism among releases. Apparently, as a place for inmates to reflect on the value of a life of crime and punishment, it wins hands down.

Many prisons today are new or modernized. Inmates enjoy housing equipped with everything from internet, gyms and college degrees, to conjugal visits. They demonstrate a clear deviation from Sher Joe's unique version of incarceration. The new model is considerably less punitive. Inmates in upscale institutions have access to more free time and leisure activities than the conditions previously associated with the term *penal institution.* Not all prisons are so nicely appointed, whether privatized or the standard government run operation. But those that are have more amenities than many ordinary, lawful citizens have or ever hope to have.

Special treatment of criminals minimizes the differences between them and us. Softening the impact of incarceration is inappropriate and misplaced compassion. It denies the whole point of removing criminals from society: punishment. It blurs the line between freedom and imprisonment. If living out a sentence isn't such a bad deal, then where is the incentive not to re-offend? Pink underwear and chain gangs incentivize. Surfing the internet and shooting hoops does not. Prisons should do everything possible to encourage the damaged human being inside the bright orange jumpsuit to become a better person. But it is sheer fantasy to believe spoiling inmates will spare society from further injury once they are released. Whether in pink or orange, one size does not fit all. Few criminals will change into productive ex-cons because few want to, and few have the character to do so. But one thing is clear: posh does not cure criminals. It coddles felons.

This is the criminal's side of the social contract: no contract at all. Its heads I win, tails you lose. Courts know it, legal and mental health counselors know it, offenders know it, and rap sheets prove it. The revolving door of the Criminal Justice System illustrates the resistance of most criminally minded people to reform. Society should reconcile with the fact that some human beings are not interested in playing by the rules; not now, not ever. They thrive on chaos, not order. Ordinary life is intolerable to a thug. Crime is much more fun than stocking shelves at Wal-Mart. To be soft on this mindset is to condone it and allow it to grow.

Martin got sideways with a family of gangsters who had no respect for life, let alone the law. The party that fateful night celebrated the release from prison and homecoming of Julio's older brother. It was also a send-off for the big-daddy of the clan, Julio's father, who was going back in for another five years. Julio was a juvenile offender who served a couple years for weapons and drugs. When he was twelve,

Julio shot and killed a younger brother during an argument. The bunch of them were a carousel of sociopaths, rotating in and out of prison like rats in a sewer.

Martin's brother served a prison sentence for drug trafficking. So did his father. A sister committed suicide while he was in prison. Years of trauma, abuse and violence festered in Martin and Julio. It fueled deep, unrequited rage. Each was the product of different circumstances and cultures. But the common denominator they shared was the serpent in the house: *domestic violence*. In the heat of rage-fueled passion, two ripened forces collided on the wall between the yards that night. Angry Martin and doped-up Julio unleashed what they knew so well. In a flash of madness, each turned a lifetime of violence against the other. Hate splattered across a hushed sky - the contract sealed for eternity. And families, neighbors and a community grieved.

Horse thieves and cattle rustlers seldom saw the inside of a courthouse in the Wild West. If you rustled cattle, you'd be tracked down and killed to get them back. If you stole a horse, you'd be hung from a tree. That was the contract of the frontier. A person's stock and mount were lifelines. Existence depended on them. It was a waste of time and a good horse to take a scoundrel to court fifty miles away. Self-preservation and survival depended on swift and effective punishment. But it was merciless, and in the wrong hands, led to vigilantism.

In time, lawlessness gave way to the Rule of Law and a more civilized form justice. We would like to believe those days of violence no longer exist in America. But they do. The news tells us so: decapitations, mutilations, shootings-every form of violence imaginable happening in our homes and cities. The case of Martin and Julio reminds us that we haven't changed much at all. We seem to be sliding back into a state of frontier lawlessness once again.

What you can do: Re-examine the contracts and agreement you have made. Look for ways to reaffirm what you believe in. Remember, you are the maker of your destiny. If we reap what we sow, then sow the very best you can.

CHAPTER 3

DENIAL

If President John F. Kennedy had denied the threat of Soviet Missiles in Cuba during the Cold War, we would speak Russian today in America. In the Cuban Missile Crisis,[1] Kennedy was willing to take military action to stop Soviet force just ninety miles from American soil. In that historic crisis we saw on one hand absolute refusal by the United States to accept the presence of Cuban missiles. On the other, Soviet Premier Khrushchev chose not to deny America's ultimatum, agreeing instead to disarm the warheads.

Denial had served two masters very well: the President and the aggressor, in two different versions of one outcome. An act of refusal by either country to accept the immutable facts they faced would have led to disaster. The United States retained national sovereignty and averted war by denying power to a regime intent on turning North America into a gulag. Soviet agreement to withdraw laid the groundwork for the end of the Cold War, and the beginning of warmer relations between the two countries.

By the 1980's, when a new Premier, Gorbachov, was poised in the Kremlin, sanitization of the old Soviet play book began. During his tenure, extensive purging of dogma and outdated leadership was conducted. New direction brought *glasnost*, the Soviet policy of better communication and transparency, and *perestroika*, a massive transformation of the Soviet political system itself. Nuclear weaponry and fierce competition for global domination increased. The world's two most powerful nations found themselves retooling their perspectives and goals to keep pace in the arms race. Nyet meant no, and no meant no, but in an era of mutual nuclear capability, stubborn differences were softening to avert conflict between the super powers.

Some decisions are non-negotiable. They are based on right and wrong. By acknowledging the force and determination of the opposition, each head of state triggered a greater sense of empowerment in the other. They were driven by a shared and terrible truth of their potential, not powered by it. Power over others is not true strength, although it may appear that way when used to control and intimidate. Rather, power is conditional because its locus of control is external. All outside sources of power are temporary. Empowerment is true strength because it is internally generated from a permanent well of energy. Like confidence, honor and integrity, it is authentic power that you own. It can never be given - or taken away without permission.

RED FLAGS

Giving people the benefit of the doubt is much less complicated than taking time and energy to check things out. Social media and the internet are fertile ground for new friendships and contacts. Without going anywhere or knowing anything about them, it is easy to gather hundreds of friends. The cyber world also tells horror stories about children and adults who are victims of crime as a result of sharing information on the internet. Not doing our homework before entrusting personal information to others is how we end up in dangerous situations. Denial of that fact is not healthy, it's stupid. Denying to give trust until it is safe to do so is a healthy use of denial. It gives us time to discriminate the facts.

Discrimination is not a bad word. To accurately discriminate is discernment, the skill by which we are able to make good decisions and judgments; to tell right from wrong. Complacency and naiveté on the other hand, open the door to potential abuse. Unfortunately, knowing when and how much to trust in any situation is not a native skill. Ignoring glaring red flags or our small inner voices warning us to be careful can get us into a whole heap of trouble. Our denial systems can be very clever and highly selective. They will kick-in with a vengeance when we really want something, making it difficult to see things clearly. Most of us know from past mistakes that wrongly placed trust, just as excessive mistrust, can bring us great unhappiness. But we may still close our minds to what we don't want to know in order to have what we want.

Gollum, a spooky Hobbit in the movie *Lord of the Rings*,[2] was a misshapen and disturbed character of incredible cunning and intelligence. With smooth talk and a piteous, self-deprecating, manner, Gollum was able to insinuate himself into positions of trust over and over again with Bilbo Baggins, a gentle Shire Hobbit. Despite Gollum's hideous appearance and obviously deranged behavior, Baggins repeatedly allows Gollum the benefit of the doubt. He even denounces his lifelong friend under Gollum's deception. Baggins was in denial. He could only see with his heart in the beginning of their travels together, not his head. Time after time he failed to discern the truth behind Gollum's attentions. At the same time, Gollum was a master of discernment. Everything Baggins did and said was studied with perfect attunement to his agenda of stealing the ring from the naïve Hobbit.

Having lost all common sense to the object of their mutual affection, "Precious," the magical gold ring, the Hobbits each became emotionally blinded to reality. Denial, deception, and distrust brought out the worst in both of them as they struggled for possession of the ring. Once under its spell, Gollum was incapable, and Baggins unwilling to see, let alone heed, the red flags foretelling their ultimate destruction.

Sadly, once we've been burned badly enough by gifting trust where it doesn't belong, we start to lose confidence in our ability to make good judgments. Self-esteem, self-trust and joy begin to disintegrate. We may find ourselves so afraid or bitter that we start holding back in life, denying ourselves what is good and enjoyable in relationships and day to day living. Love may be blind, but denial, in some cases doesn't even have eyes.

VODKA, VIOLENCE, AND IWONKA

Immigrants coming to America seeking political asylum from regimes that persecute and imprison people on trumped up or unjust charges arrive here in a state of shock. Iwonka, a frail, pale, middle-aged woman and her family had been in the U.S. less than a year. She and her husband, Boris, and two children had left Russia because he had gotten involved with some small time hoodlums and was about to be arrested for armed robbery. Boris was not guilty, according to Iwonka, even though his were the only fingerprints found on the gun that was used in the crime. The hoods ratted him out making him their scapegoat.

Sponsored and funded by a large community of ex-Soviet and Russian Americans, the entire family was able to escape from their homeland and begin a new life of freedom in Arizona. Iwonka and the children would be free at last of the modern version of the KGB. But they were not free from Boris' consumption of vodka, or the horrible abuse and fear that chilled the blood in their veins. Utter terror welled up in Iwonka's eyes and shook her body as she cautiously walked into my office and sat down for our initial evaluation.

Speaking in very broken English, she nervously told me about the incident - her arrest for shoplifting. "I had to do it, he was going to beat the boy if I didn't do it for him!" she cried, pleading her innocence. The court documents she handed me showed she had been cited for theft at Walgreens the week before. Her face turned bright red as she continued in a louder and more heavily accented voice: "Please, Miss, please, please don't let them send me and my kids back! We die. They kill us if we go back! My boy and girl, they go to orphanage. KGB put me in work camp!" Sobbing and shaking replaced her caution as she begged me for mercy.

I felt sickened by the woman's plea for her life, and the lives of her children. I had seen East German ghettos, and Soviet guards with machine guns pointed at me from a hundred meters away. I observed them from the West side, the free side of Berlin, during the Cold War years. Those experiences were blood-curdling. What Iwonka had been through, I could not begin to fathom. As she sat before me, it was clear she was in crisis. She was suffering from Posttraumatic Stress Disorder (PTSD).[3] Iwonka was anxious and paranoid.

It was difficult to calm her down and explain that she was not going to be sent back to Russia. City Court was not KGB. They had simply referred her to counseling after reviewing her unusual case. Walgreens wasn't going to exact their usual fine for restitution. Mercy had already been granted, but Iwonka didn't seem to understand that as she sat in front of me shivering with shame and fear. What troubled me were the facts of her case. Iwonka, the wife and mother of two young children, had shoplifted a gallon of vodka from the drugstore.

Iwonka was kicked out of their apartment by Boris, who had flown into a rage because he used up the last bottle he had in the apartment. She was ordered to go get him more. "And," the woman stumbled, "that I not to come home without, or he beats me, and he beats children again…that he will beats us…with razor strap!" My jaw clenched as she spoke those words. She said *again*-beats us *again* with a razor strap. There was much more to her anguish than having been caught smuggling a large bottle of alcohol out of a liquor store. Iwonka and her children were victims of domestic violence. Nobody knew. She was petrified that it would be found out. In her mind, it would get her deported, so she and the children kept it secret, just like they had in Russia.

Alcoholism had been just a way of life in her world. After all, she added, " water bad in Minsk, it make you sick, so you drink something, da?" She never touched a drop herself, but Boris and his friends, in fact, everyone they knew back home was a drunk. Beating your wife and kids was expected in the insanity of post-Soviet Russia. Her family was sick, living a life of monstrous pain and misery. That hadn't changed by virtue of coming to America. But Iwonka was busted for stealing booze to prevent physical injury to herself and the children. Her shoplifting and arrest changed everything. She never imagined that one singular act of survival could, finally, give her the freedom she came here for.

Our work together was going to be a very steep climb. The post-Soviet culture in which Iwonka and Boris grew up and raised their children came with them to America. Violence expressed in their home and country was turned loose as soon as they arrived. Their damaged children acted out in school and developed stress-related illnesses. They were angry, lonely and abused kids until Iwonka's fortunate arrest brought them to a new beginning.

Iwonka left Boris and found safety with her children in a women's shelter. Months later, I had the pleasure of seeing her again. After many hours of family and individual therapy, the little Russian family of three was slowly coming to life. With support and education, Iwonka and the children were able to realize how strong they were and how bright their future was. It would take years to dispose of the garbage that had collected in their souls. The scars would remain. But every day they began to replace trauma with joy and laughter. Iwonka was a re-born woman; the children were young and resilient. The progression of violence in Iwonka's children was interrupted, and anger was redirected. Mother and children broke the cycle of generational violence that was once all they knew. Because they denied violence continued power over them, they moved on to healthy, loving lives.

DENIAL AND GRIEF

Instinct and intuition are important for making good choices. Neither of them lie. They are natural reservoir that speak the truth. Together they form a skillset that can override emotions and the stubbornly embedded tentacles of denial. It is no coincidence that renowned psychiatrist, Elizabeth Kuebler-Ross,[4] placed denial first in identifying the five stages of grief. In her work on death and dying, she observed how some children and adults devastated by trauma slipped into a protective state of numbness. Being sealed off from reality deflects the impact of a debilitating event. It is a natural response to pain.

Humans don't process grief in the same way. The capacity to withstand and recover from trauma is unique to each of us. We don't usually know exactly how we will handle crisis until it happens. The emotional desolation of grief and loss can be so profound it may even kill us. It is not uncommon to hear of grieving spouses succumbing to their own deaths shortly after the loss of their mates. Love and partnership build bonds so strong we may be grievously lost when someone cherished dies. After seventy years of marriage, my long-lived and healthy grandfather died of 'natural causes' less than three weeks after his wife. Animal companions often become depressed and lose vitality after the death of a beloved master. Shock is brutal.

For some people, survival depends on this ability to temporarily shut down. Shock allows us to linger in limbo for a while - a state of suspended animation in which we are neither here nor there. We are emotionally unavailable. Immobilization conserves energy that will be needed to overcome suffering. Denial is unconscious lying that allows us to avoid the truth. It pads the journey from grief to acceptance. Kuebler-Ross witnessed this reaction to loss and recognized it as the onset of the healing process. As we move into the second stage of grief we encounter rage. Although agonizing, it is a critical step. Anger begins the pattern of blistering that brings oxygen to open wounds because we are out from under the anesthetic of denial.

In the third stage, called bargaining, we cycle through an emotional wringer. It stirs up irrational beliefs that lead us to try and rationalize, or "bargain" our way out of grief. But it doesn't work. Hopeless and exhausted, we sink into despair. Unless we are able to see a glimmer of hope for an end to our misery, we will become very depressed. This is the most dangerous stage. Risk of suicide is highest. Victims of violence like Iwonka are especially at risk of dying when they are catapulted into the stages of grief. Depression is often compounded by other factors such as fear and post-trauma stress from abuse. For victims of violence, it is all or nothing. They will either stay stuck in the trauma, return to the abuser, or leave. Oscar Christensen, one of my university professors said it simply: "if you're not there it can't happen!" When Iwonka finally awakened from her nightmare, she entered the final stage of grief: *acceptance.* It is the opposite of denial. Acceptance embraces the truth and rejects the lie. She never looked back.

TANGLED WEB

Intentional deception is a different kind of denial. Everyone lies a little now and then, but continuous manipulation of the truth violates trust and destabilizes relationships. Chronic liars love top dog status and will fabricate or embellish the truth to get it. Pathological liars are a menace to relationships and society because they are without conscience. They are remorseless snake oil vendors who defraud others for personal benefit. The brightest of these actors are able to hide their tangled web of lies. But once discovered, they try to walk back their dishonesty and smooth over the ruffled feathers of their victims. If that fails, there are always other fish to fry. Liars happily move on to the next sucker.

Persistent lying is cowardice, so abusive relationships are especially favorite lairs for liars. It is common for a batterer to be one person at home, and another in public. When police are called to a domestic problem, abusers carefully distort their roles in the conflict. They will stop at nothing to save their backsides. And fearing the abuse they'll suffer if they talk, victims clam up. Abusers can be charming. They know that most people don't want to believe the nice person they know in public is a vile beast at home. We don't want to butt into other people's business, and don't want anyone in ours. But when it comes to violence, silence is a form of collusion. Denial and silence enable violence.

Quantum physics, the Theory of Relativity, tells us that what we see in the physical world is not permanent. It is only a snapshot of that activity or image in the moment of time that we are looking at it. What we see is not the whole or "steady state" picture of its potential. Everything is relative. A great deal about the energy of a given entity is unknown and unpredictable, as it cannot be seen all the time in every way possible. The theory accurately describes the typical criminal in general, but it is especially true of perpetrators of abuse and violence. It is hard to imagine the full potential of that which is unknown or invisible in anyone, let alone, someone capable of violence. True sociopaths don't divulge the rabbits they hold in their hat until they pull them out.

When children are subjected to domestic or societal violence, their tender souls are assaulted. Kids in the worst of these warzones learn to stuff their thoughts and feelings to stay alive. They learn the rules and become keepers of the lie. Without safety and protection, everything precious and cherished about being a child is destroyed by violence. Intervention can't happen when abuse is cloaked in silence and nobody talks. Perhaps good intentions and respect for privacy cause people to mind their own business. Maybe it's just a little argument like we all have occasionally, we say to ourselves when we hear quarreling. Or we fear getting hurt ourselves by stepping in to help someone. Whatever the reason, abuse and violence thrive because of the unwillingness of so many to call for help.

Sons who witness their mothers being abused are extremely vulnerable to becoming violent themselves. A child is unable to fend off an abuser. Little boys unable to protect their mothers carry the anger and shame of their perceived inadequacy into adulthood. A son may go through life unable to forgive himself, the abuser, or even his mother. After all, he may decide, she is the reason he was put to shame. If she hadn't allowed the abuser to be in the home, the violence wouldn't have happened. He is traumatized and reeling in anger. Mostly mothers raise sons. When angry sons go out into the world and develop relationships they are at risk of repeating the violence they've witnessed. Especially with women.

Childhood memories of abuse become adult patterns of behavior for millions of people exposed to violence as children. Family violence is a chain of pathology that is carried from generation to generation. It is easy to understand how it also forms the basis of societal violence. The serpent takes on many forms, but it's still the same beast. Whether in the home or on the street, violence is violence. Most children walk the path they have been shown. It's the path they know. When it is one of violence, it will continue until another way is learned. Tolerance for criminal behavior a learned response to violence.

TOLERANCE

One of the most dangerous forms of denial known to mankind is *tolerance*. Tolerance is the willingness or capacity to accept something we don't necessarily agree with. If something is intolerable it is normally rejected, not accepted. When there is conflict between acceptable and intolerable, denial comes in to play. Denial is a compromise which allows tolerance. Even if denial is the result of apathy, stupidity, or ignorance, it is permission, just the same. Ignorance is a poor excuse for immorality.

In the early 1940's, farmers and townsfolk in Germany went about the normal business of their lives. For years, Germans lived under a heavy blanket of toxic smoke. It belched from the crematoriums of Nazi death camps that were scattered across the *Vaterland*. The darkness filled the sky and their lungs with the unmistakable stench of incinerated human flesh. By developing an ability to *tolerate the smell of murder*, thousands of people were capable of ignoring the horrors taking place in their backyards. It is one of the most heinous examples of denial and tolerance. Ironically, *intolerance* was the underlying psychopathy that funded *the Holocaust*.[5]

Intelligent intolerance, on the other hand, could manifest good for mankind. Ending the enrichment of uranium and the development of warheads by deranged sociopaths would be wise. When elected leaders tolerate behaviors that jeopardize our personal and national security, it is a trickle-down threat to all of us. Without the enforcement of boundaries and laws, our borders, cities, streets and households are not safe. America is at critical mass. Our angry streets and people tell the story of a nation in crisis, not good health and prosperity

We are at a tipping point in our short history. America is an unrecognizable caricature of itself. We have lost the vitality and integrity that once made us whole. National pride has been replaced with separatism and divisiveness. Special interest groups and a mentality of entitlement have demeaned individualism, hard work, and American exceptionalism. There is a new cultural ideal, one that moves us away from the moral standards of our founding fathers and immigrant ancestors. It is a toxic cocktail of government expansion, pop culture, and political correctness. This is a serpent of another kind. It is dismantling our country by encouraging dependence and discouraging achievement. Crisis is a fertile environment for violence.

MIRRORS

The skulls of our club-dragging ancestors increased in size during thousands of years of evolution. As information was gathered and new skills were learned, humans needed more space for their expanding brains. Through generations of mankind, patterns of memories, skills and experiences are inherited and handed down in families and society. In Jungian psychology, this accumulation of knowledge and experience is called the collective unconscious.[5] It is the collective mind of humankind. Concepts such as spirituality, science, and morality expand in the collective mind. They enable survival, progress and happiness. A déjà vu moment may be the recollection of an archetypal memory from our vast, ancestral databank. This is especially true of dreams and behavior, which Jung believed are affected by these ancient patterns of memories.

Humans didn't make it this far being stupid or in denial about life. Early man used instinct and brute force to survive a life that was short, stressful, and very violent. Existence depended on cooperation between clan members, formidable skills, and a keen attunement with nature. This is intelligence. The Man in the Ice,[6] was discovered in the Swiss Alps in 1991. The body was well-preserved from the ice and snow he died in five-thousands of years ago in the Stone Age. His tools, clothes, hair, and DNA reveal the kind of life he lived and who he was genetically. Scientists believe he was murdered. History tells us that violence has, and will continue to be a fact of life for mankind. The question is whether we will use our collective intelligence to manage it.

Our ancestral tribes were ingenious, vigilant and tough, or you wouldn't be reading this book. These are the clans from which we originate. Because of their extraordinary adaptability, we are here to do and become almost anything we set our minds to. The first place to correct the problems that impact our lives is at home. Our families provide the best opportunity to witness how we deal with anger and conflict. A home has many mirrors, and each tells a different story about your life. Go look and see what is there.

We are blessed with the ability to think, feel, and respond to our environment, not only react. The world is a dangerous place. Few of us have the finely tuned instincts of the ice man, the stamina and sleuth of the Vikings, or the survival skills of the American pioneer. Instead, we are dependent on our ability to think and reason. We have intelligent, collective minds. We have the wisdom and courage of our ancient fathers and mothers. Reinforcing our families is the key to rebuilding our nation.

Chicago is one of the world's most dangerous cities. The South Side is an ugly and heartbreaking reflection of the failure to protect the innocent and prosecute the guilty. It is a city in crisis with unstoppable crime and violence. In a recent report on almost one hundred cities, Chicago came in last for enforcement of the law. Local and national media are either muzzled or indifferent, because too many crimes go unreported in the news. Chicago is the poster child for legalized crime. Refusal by city and state government to control the problem is bewildering.

Is this an example of denial? No, and yes. Everybody in Illinois knows how bad it is in Chicago. Ask the elders, the mothers, and the children of the South Side what their lives are like. There is slaughter on the streets and playgrounds every day. The carnage persists without interruption and no sign of compassion. The city is in denial because it fails to stop the blood bath. Officials glance away as mothers wail over the murder of a child or misguided teen. Gangs, money, and drugs rule the street, not law and order. Families are in crisis.

Several miles due north, the famous North Shore glitters along the curves of Lake Michigan. The 'Magnificent Mile' is lined with upscale boutiques and historic landmarks. Pricey high rise apartments, hotels, restaurants and office buildings shimmer with light and bustle with activity day and night. Lake Shore Drive creates the stunning silhouette that is Chicago's signature. This is the beautiful, affluent side of Chicago. But despite the glitz and great pizza, Chicago is Murder City. "Chi-town" has long been an incubator of corruption and crime. Like Detroit, it is a vulgar reminder of why we as a country need to enforce the Rule of Law and reaffirm family values. Both cities are the result of denial, tolerance, and the loss of American ideals. They are examples of everything wrong in our culture.

BEARERS OF VIRTUE

Denial and tolerance are not options if we want to save our country. Pink underwear and chain gangs work better than sympathy in the world of crime and punishment. Yet, many courts and legislators dole out leniency and forgiveness to criminals like cookies at an ice cream social. It is counterintuitive to a reasoned mind that special treatment should be granted to the guilty. Tolerance of crime and soft enforcement of the law are counterproductive to our wellbeing as a society. They encourage crime. America can reasonably expect a worsening of the crime rate if we continue to soften the definition, prosecution and consequences of crime.

Rejection and denial of reason leads to disorder. The Supreme Court of the United States decided in favor of forcing the State of California to release nearly ten thousand dangerous felons from crowded prisons back into society. By virtue of this ruling, millions of Americans are exposed to the worst kinds of criminals as inmates flood out of prison and into our neighborhoods. There were other options, like re-housing in the forty-nine other states in the country, for example. This kind of reasoning by our highest and most trusted Court is a violation of our right to protection under the Constitution. It sets a precedent for the release of criminals from other prisons around the country. Society is at greater risk when criminals realize they may not have to serve time for crimes committed.

Americans are blessed with certain inalienable rights. Denial of those rights is illegal and immoral. When the Obama administration set up an email "snitch line" in 2009, it created a furor. The purpose of the website, flag@whitehouse.gov, was to collect the identities of opponents of healthcare. Americans were asked to email the names of friends, neighbors, family and anyone else they knew disagreed with White House policies. The website was (allegedly) quietly shut down shortly after it was advertised to the public. Collection and storage of such tips' and information by a President is a violation of the federal Privacy Act of 1974.[7] But the damage was done. Information was received and stored. This shocking attempt to intimidate Americans who are exercising their Constitutional rights is a wakeup call we better not ignore.

Enlisting Americans to 'snitch' smacks of Soviet Union and KGB. It is not the American way. Activists for social justice advance their agenda of fairness in this atmosphere of intolerance. Dissent is not tolerated, it is punished. This is justice, it is *selective injustice*. Selective tolerance is phony tolerance. It defiles the true essence of fairness by which most ordinary people endeavor to live. Social justice has been twisted into a password for morality, but it is spineless hypocrisy. This kind of injustice is amorality - a graceless state without morals. True morality has virtue, and virtue is not conditional. No country has endured without morals, virtue, and justice. Social order depends on these higher elements of consciousness. Without the discipline and enforcement of laws, humans do not reach their full potential. But when laws are applied unequally it is tyranny.

Our lives are impacted by many social conditions over which we have little or no control. When those conditions are stressful, our lives are more stressed. Abuse of power takes place in relationships, society and government. It inflames anger and creates a sense of helplessness. Sooner or later, the stress it causes builds up and is unleashed as violence. Denial allows the cycle to continue. There is a commonality between politics and crime. In both there is no chance of survival by minding *only* one's business. Players on these stages have their fingers on the pulse of the enemy at all times. *Know thine enemy*, the saying goes. Lose the pulse, and life as you knew it is over. This is the rationale behind espionage, surveillance and war. It is also what drives corruption.

What you can do: Take care to protect your rights, freedoms, and privacy. Develop a keen sense of awareness and reject denial as a hiding place. Understand but don't fear the challenges we face as a culture. Create a sense of safety, security, and joy in your world and take each day one at a time. Draw on the wisdom of history and the consciousness of your tribe for strength and courage.

CHAPTER 4

MIND YOUR OWN BUSINESS

"If you keep telling my wife lies about me and putting all that f-----g garbage in her stupid head you're gonna be sorry!" the pencil-scrawled letter began. "She is becoming a problem for me because of you, so you are becoming a big problem for me! Get it?" The man's barely legible rant continued. "I put that c---t in the hospital like the piece-of-trash-s--t she is, and I can do the same to you too, you stupid f-----g b---h!" Damon, my name for him, clearly was not cooking on all four burners when he decided to send a letter threatening to harm his wife's court-ordered counselor. That is, of course, if Damon, Jennifer's husband, had in fact actually penned the warning.

With almost fifteen years of practice as a psychotherapist under my belt, I had never been threatened. That is amazing, considering the population I worked with consisted primarily of referrals from the Criminal Justice System on charges of domestic violence and substance abuse. Both were potentially dangerous to my health, but prior to this letter, I had never felt that my safety was at risk.

But an entire letter had been dedicated to inflicting fear in me, and I took it seriously: "I know where you work, where you live, and what kind of car you drive"…it read, "I can make you disappear -

far away where no one will ever find you! It's a big lonely desert out there, [really bad word for woman here]!" Indeed, it was a vast and treacherous desert beyond the bright lights of the city. Over the years, many people suspected of being murdered had suddenly disappeared from this overgrown cow-town. Most of their bodies and killers were never found. There was no doubt in my mind that this man had the ability to carry out his threat to harm.

The last paragraph of the letter made the point: "You're stickin' your big nose in family business where it shouldn't be, and you and all them cops and f-----g judges and lawyers are butting in where you don't belong. We don't do business with you pigs." The last sentence read: "Stop seeing her…or you and her, you two b-----s both go down! You hear me? *Down!*"

I picked up the phone and called 911. It was after 9:00, and the entire building was empty as I waited alone in my office for the police to arrive. Fortunately, what seemed like an hour had been less than ten minutes before two officers knocked on my office door. As they took my report and read the letter, a deep unsettling fear began to numb my senses. With a terrifying chill that sent shivers through my body I heard myself thinking: Am I being stalked by my own killer? The sky was pitch black and the air was freezing cold when they walked me down the stairs to my car in the dimly lit parking lot.

The squad car followed behind me for a few miles. I felt better and the presence in my rear view mirror eased my grip on the steering wheel for a while. Then they were gone. My bones rattled uncontrollably the rest of the way home. I was afraid of what might be in store for me if this guy went nuts and hunted me down. Even after the police got a warrant issued for his arrest, Damon's letter never left my thoughts. Spouses, families and jilted lovers are rife with resentment and unpredictability when one of them is brought to justice, fairly or unfairly. Soiled linen is not for public display in the dangerous world of crime and violence. People go to very nasty ends to prevent the exposure of secrets. Jennifer went missing. I imagined this was how inconvenient people in their world got eliminated. I prayed I wasn't next.

There are no surprises in the work of a counselor. Anything and everything is possible. In the end, Damon was not the author of the threatening letter to me. He had enough trouble of his own and was looking at hard time for battering his wife. On this particular rap, he was clean. It was another family member, Zeke, "el Zorro" (the fox), who decided to take the problem with Jennifer into his own hands. He was a convicted felon on the run for attempted murder.

Zeke wanted to shut up the tattling wife and scare me out of the picture. In his mind, Jennifer knew too much, too much family 'business,' and needed to be muzzled. As her confidant, I also needed to be silenced. Fortunately, that was not to happen; at least, not to me. Zeke got busted for a DUI and went back to prison. I will probably never know what happened to Jennifer. Confiding in me about her violent husband and marriage may have cost Jennifer her life. No one talked.

EAVESDROPPING

What we used to consider personal and private has gone forever public. With or without our permission, anyone can find out just about everything about us. Purchasing and renting a home or office, applying for a job, and going to school will trigger a credit score and a background check. Virtually nothing is off-limits. All of our laundry, clean and dirty, hangs out there permanently exposed. Twenty-four hours, seven days a week around the world, privacy is gone. Fifty years ago, a background check was called a Mercantile. Verification of personal and financial information was limited to select organizations and legal authorities. It was considered rude if not intrusive to run an investigation on an individual or group without a legitimate reason. Privacy was respected, and what was called "common decency" prohibited the exploitation of personal information. *Times have changed.*

Americans face the single greatest threat to our Constitution we have ever known: *the warrantless surveillance, retrieval, and storage by the Federal Government of every bit of personal information about us that currently and ever will exist.* Federal data collection programs like PRISM (Planning Tool for Resource Integration, Synchronization, and Management), and the NSA (National Security Agency), may have unlimited access to every detail our lives. Everything we think, feel, say, do, as well as who we know can be monitored. The tip line for snitching was just a tip of this very deep iceberg.

Der Spiegel (the mirror), a weekly news magazine published in Hamburg, Germany, reported that these agencies can access data on most smart phones including contact lists, texts, emails and location..[1] Britain and the US have set up teams to "crack" the protective devices on these phones. Read that again: *our smart phones came equipped with protective devices, presumably to protect our Constitutional rights to privacy. Now, suddenly, we no longer have those rights?* We are being treated more like pawns and puppets than human beings by our own government. Everything and everyone has become someone else's business. Sound-amplification technology al lowing people to listen in on conversations are easy to buy and use.

Social halls in old European castles have eaves. An eave is the part of the ceiling that meets and overhangs the wall. Wood carvings of human heads were hung from these edifices high above the tables and chairs usually filled with guests. Paranoia and fear surrounded royalty and their courts in those days. The bizarre caricatures were intended to remind gossiping courtiers and traitors that their secrets might be overheard. As a result of this practice, 'eavesdropping' has come to mean listening-in on conversations. Sadly, our lives today are full of real eavesdroppers, not wood carvings. Plundering the privacy of others is a form of trespass. And when our personal space is violated, it makes us mad.

While some use it for ulterior motives, technology has also provided us with immeasurable entertainment and information. People, places and experiences stream to life before our eyes. The gifts of technology are magical antidotes to just about anything that troubles us. Music streams into our consciousness and fills our senses with the timeless lyric of the ages as we download our favorite tunes. Videos transport us to far-away places, and social media connects us to the world. We can feel the mood shift in our souls. It is Nirvana; but it is temporary. In those moments of contentment and timelessness at the keyboard, the rabid streets of Chicago and the drug traffickers across town are a million miles away. All that matters is the next text, phone call, email or media post. But we are in *denial.*

Videos and photos uploaded to the web from around the world have shown us the stoning deaths of women, beheadings of journalists, the real-time ravages of war and crime, people shoved to their deaths onto subway tracks, torture, graphic sex and child pornography. Nothing is *verboten* or taboo. As if we don't have enough horrible news and graphics from our own country, we can tune into vile visuals from around the world. But even though it's real stuff we're looking at, *it's not our stuff.* So we hunker down on our computers, see what we want, and reject what we don't. Click, it's gone. Out of sight, out of mind. Unless it clangs a specific gong in our heads or hearts, or takes a bite out of our own lives or pocketbooks, most of us just don't pay attention to the business of this tired, run-down country we call home. It's boring and someone else's problem. Living for the moment is more fun. It is also how we ignore the violence-creep imbedding itself in our culture. From the highest offices of government, to abused spouses, murdered children, and acts of terrorism, America is under assault.

BUTTERFLIES AND SURFERS

Many Americans are content not only to let someone else take care of the business of our country, but to take care of them as well. At this writing, being taken care of is the mainstay of some fifteen million Americans on food stamps, and ninety million that have left the workforce. High unemployment and a near zero gross domestic product are staggering reflections of the distressed state of our nation.

Yet, unbelievably, we continue to spiral down the rabbit hole of financial ruin while ignoring the reasons why.

Most people don't understand the collateral damage associated with being taken care of by the government. In science there is something called the *Butterfly Theory of Chaos.*[2] When a change takes place in the natural order of something it sets off a series of changes and adaptations in others affected by that change. The delicate balance between them has been altered, forcing a new behavior to replace the lost one. Sometimes new behavior is fraught with panic and stress because of the difficulty of the process of adaptation. But in time, the adjustment will be made, and life will go on. Many able-bodied people deny responsibility for their own care. Allowing the social system to take care of them is easier than adapting to losses or changes in their lives. Fraudulent entitlement breeds laziness and abuse. It prevents personal growth and self-esteem. It is an unnecessary expense everyone else ends up paying.

A cable news station interviewed an unemployed, twenty-something California surfer/musician living on welfare. His story quickly went viral on the internet. The lobster-eating, self-avowed ladies' man on Food Stamps also drives a big SUV. This is a sad example of wrongful entitlement. Asked what he would want to say to the taxpayers who are paying for his free-loading lifestyle, he flashes a wide smile, cocks his head to one side and responds: *"Thanks, taxpayers!"* Those are not the sentiments of a responsible adult. They are the attributes of a thief, not of character. Only swindlers and drug users feel good about theft. The rest of us feel ripped off and angry.

At some point, the entitlement gravy train will be empty. There will be no Uncle Sam sugar-daddy to take care of people like the surfer. Multitudes of grifters will find themselves sinking in the quicksand of our national bankruptcy. If we fail to stop the entitlement bleed, people in genuine need may find themselves destitute. Economic crises lead to social chaos, and that means crime and violence.

There is a philosophical difference between the terms 'caretaking,' and 'caregiving'. They are not interchangeable and are often misused and misunderstood. To "take care of" means to assume responsibility for the care of. It is an act of taking control. In a civil society, compassionate people take care of the old, the disabled, orphans, and those who are severely disadvantaged. People incapable of taking care of themselves exist in every culture. Few would argue that reality. In these cases, care-taking doesn't replace someone's ability to care for themselves. They don't *have* the ability to care for themselves.

In dysfunctional relationships and families, however, the person described as "caretaker" bears a negative connotation. Relationship caretakers have an inordinate need to control. They over-assume responsibility in order to please others and maintain their position of importance. Because caretakers never say no, they allow themselves to be used and abused in the name of loyalty or love. But micro-managing others never wins brownie points. It creates animosity. When family members feel suffocated they start to rebel, and the devoted caretaker becomes angry and resentful. If they feel unappreciated and taken advantage of, caretakers see themselves as victims. The Victim's Triangle is in play, and conflict is inevitable as the relationship slips out of balance.

Care-giving is a supportive action that affirms strengths and abilities, instead of inabilities. The words "giving" and "taking" illustrate the difference between the two types of care. Caregiving is respectful and encourages independence. Skills and abilities are augmented with new ones geared toward self-care. Emergency government assistance was designed to provide temporary relief to people in distress. Welfare was not intended to take care of millions of capable people unwilling to work. Hard-working taxpayers are abused by the big business of universal caretaking. Massive entitlements leach prosperity from the honest. It is dirty money in the hands of the dishonest. This is social violence of another kind. Tolerance of abuse is a choice.

Minding our business is a complicated issue. Abuse of the welfare system is everybody's business and everybody's problem. Social caretaking is one of the problems enabling the decline of our culture. Rescuing people instead of inspiring self-sufficiency creates victims. When we allow ourselves to be victimized, we are contributing to our own violation.

UNDENIABLE TRUTHS

Over the past few decades, it has become popular to look outside our borders to spend money. Billions of dollars are sent to countries that hate and attack us. But we keep the bucks flowing even while millions of people in America live in crisis. We don't make it our priority to take care of our own first. Courts allow greater freedom to use drugs and release criminals back into society. Dangerous cities breed violence, and unsecured borders put communities in harm's way. This is the opposite of government taking care of its people. It is taking care away. The population is dumbing down because of low expectation and greater dependency. By extracting self-esteem, independence, hope, individuality and self-determination from people, we discourage and enslave them. Compassionate humans want others to succeed and be self-reliant, not see them turned into state-owned zombies.

As a short-lived nation we haven't done everything right, but we haven't been all wrong, either. Like a beautiful doe in the headlights, we are stunned by the vehicle of social decline bearing down on us. Unlike the Statue of Liberty promising liberty and justice for all, we are blinded by what is correct and ignoring what is morally right. There is no justice in subjective liberty. We are getting whacked by our inability to recognize tyranny when it is staring us in the face.

The home of the free and the brave has not been minding her own business. The un-tended store has been looted and ransacked. With trillions in debt, spending grievously out of control, and printing money like there's no tomorrow, we give more to the rest of the world than to our own communities. As a consequence, the core of our existence- hard work, the Constitution, and the family, is being obliterated. A new ethic has been contrived to replace the pursuit of happiness, freedom, independence and self-reliance once cherished. It is not who we thought we were, and not who we want to be. Millions of people are duped by hand-outs and enticements they think are free. They are wrong. There is no free lunch. The cost is cultural decay. Humans are whole beings. Mind, spirit and body need nourishment in order to thrive. Personal fulfillment from an honest job and a life well-lived feeds the soul. Contribution to society, not a disabled life of subsidy, builds a healthy country.

THE SHUNNING

Once upon a time in America, people joined hands, horses, families, and money to help one another. They raised barns and harvested crops, bore children and buried the dead. Families and communities shared responsibility, hard work, and sheer determination. We oozed tenacity and 'stick-to-itiveness,' and no thing or person has taken us down. America gave her fathers, sons, mothers and daughters when the dogs of war were at the door. Ours is a heart of courage not even the Civil War could destroy. We have survived, no matter what. But we are a different people in a different time now. America was founded by ingenious, resourceful people bound together in commitment to faith, family, and flag. *Today, we are a country that increasingly shuns commitment to faith, family and flag.* Toughness of spirit and strength of family have softened to a shapeless bowl of jelly. Without our driving engine, the family, we are adrift in a sea of calamity, on a ship with no captain.

Former First Lady, retired Secretary of State Hillary Rodham Clinton, reportedly traveled more extensively during her years in public office than any of her predecessors. As the highest ranking representative of the President and the United States, it was her *business* to hold counsel with world leaders. It was not her job to cure the world's maladies, nor was it her business in most cases to try. Madam Secretary's globe trekking took her from the opulence of European royalty to the horrific poverty of undeveloped countries.

Third World conditions exist right here, in the bosom of America. We just don't hear much about them. People don't plan vacations to inner-city ghettos or the slums of our outback. They are realities we don't want to experience. Detroit, Chicago, New Orleans, Milwaukee, Philadelphia, Los Angeles, and many other cities are inundated with drugs, violence and corruption. Gangs, dealers and wrecking balls dominate city landscapes that were once flourishing neighborhoods. Statistically, you have a greater chance of being killed today in the city of Chicago than in the Afghan War.

Societal violence is cultural, relational, political and social. America is the most richly endowed and freest country on the planet. People come here from around the world to begin a new life and achieve their dreams. We don't have kings or elect dictators who plunder our wealth for their own coffers. Ours is not a country of genocide, ethnic cleansing, or ongoing civil war. America has no excuse for the deplorable state of her crumbling cities and the demise of her culture. We have no one to blame but our own apathy, ignorance, and failure for the crumbling of our society.

Poverty and economic stress are key predictors of relationship conflict and societal violence. The stress of joblessness, homelessness, and inability to provide the most basic human needs for oneself and children is unbearably painful. People trapped in desperate circumstances get depressed and panicky. They are more likely to use drugs and alcohol in an attempt to medicate the pain of their lives. As hopelessness and helplessness intensify, many lash out in anger. Each passing day increases frustration and anxiety until it escalates to an intolerable point of anguish. Distressed people are most vulnerable to the cycle of violence when anger, stress, and frustration spin out of control.

When domestic conflict escalates in a violent neighborhood, there is an even greater risk of injury and death. Chaos on the street aggravates violence in the home by creating a constant state of tension and anxiety. Over time, the degree of separation between private and public violence fades. Domestic violence can't be contained or remain a secret forever. The bully must come out. Sooner or later, angry people are going to act-out in public. It is the nature of perpetrators of abuse to be abusive. *Relationship violence, like every other addiction, is a lifestyle.* On the street, however, violence is an entire *culture*. The more abusive a person is, the more desensitized he is to future acts of violence. And the more desensitized become his victims.

THE LEARNING CURVE

Very few people are born angry. The exception is a baby born under the influence of its mother's addiction. An addicted newborn endures a violently painful detox in the first days of life. The infant is in acute pain as he begins what should have been a sweet, precious new life. It's easy to imagine why an addicted newborn is enraged.

Humans learn through trial and error along life's bumpy road. But for sociopaths and psychopaths, the learning curve is especially swift. They adapt quickly to the world around them because of their insatiable quest for power. All pathological behavior is anti-social, but the amount of damage it causes varies. Pathology coalesces with opportunity. And unfortunately, true sociopaths rarely miss the opportunity to exploit in one form or another.

Once it explodes, pent up rage is defused, but the terrifying effect it has on others remains imprinted in their memory. Once an explosive individual sees the cowering fear and submission his outburst causes in his victim, his power and control is established. As the cycle is repeated, power is reinforced, and the relationship gets sicker and sicker. This is true in domestic relationships, social relationships, and wherever abuse is the vehicle of control. It is what defines violence. This is the premise of *Serpent in the House*. Escalation of social violence in our culture today is a direct result of the violence occurring in our primary and domestic relationships. And the level of violence in our families and relationships intensifies as a result of the increase in societal violence.

Relationship violence may be subtle and unseen, but it is violence nonetheless. There may be no outward physical signs of trauma.

Our souls are invisible. But traumas wound us deeply. Studies reveal that the most damaging violence is that which is inflicted against the human spirit. Forms of abuse including humiliation, threats, intimidation, verbal, and emotional abuse leave no visual wounds. Sexual abuse, injury, damage, kidnap, and the harm of children and pets are examples of assault that is visible.

Hospitals and first responders are trained to watch for signs of domestic violence. But injuries are not always easy to identify as relationship caused, even for professionals. Victims often lie about what happened to them out of fear of further violence from their abuser and, *shame.* Shame and embarrassment are sources of extra pain for victims of violence. "How could any normal person allow themselves to be hurt like that? They must like it," is the common response from uninformed bystanders.

Even those we would, or should expect to understand the complexities of violence show ignorance. A high-ranking politician recently referred to "a garden variety slap on the face" as "not (being) real domestic violence". The older statesman grew up watching movies in which men and women hit each other matter-of-factly. In many classic films, women were slapped, shoved or thrown around like rag dolls. Actors shoved pies and fists in each other's faces in the name of comedy. Domestic violence as a crime didn't exist; it was in the shadows. Maybe only a hard, upper cut to the chin or punch in the eye qualifies as *real* Domestic Violence in his mind.

This is the perspective that enables violence to continue because it denies the seriousness of all violent behavior. Just like any other addiction, the abuse addict moves along a continuum that becomes increasingly worse with each incident. To depict any form of violence as '*not-as-bad- as*' another is a dishonor to the thousands of women, children, and men who are injured, dead, or murdered as a result of Domestic Violence. Failure to use his national pulpit as a vehicle of public education reinforces abuse. Little mention was made about the statement. Mainstream media, Feminists, and practitioners who treat victims of domestic violence were silent. Silence is acceptance. It was a missed opportunity to draw much needed attention to the subject. Worse, it illustrates the casual if not flip attitude toward domestic abuse prevalent in our culture.

High profile cases of domestic violence and domestic homicides take place all over the country. But domestic violence is not being connected to the overall violence in America. The two are connected. This is important business we as a society should be minding. But we don't. We shun conversations about domestic violence, and in shunning, we tolerate it. In tolerating it, we are co-creators of the monster that is the serpent in the house. Hurt and angry people make hurt and angry neighbors, employers, employees, teachers, bullies, thugs, and every other kind of person in society. We all have a breaking point. Many people have lost confidence in what tomorrow will bring in their lives and in our country. While we've been minding the business of the rest of the world, we have forgotten the most important people in the world: *us.*

What you can do: Take a deep breath and breathe in life. Every day is a new beginning and an opportunity to finely tune your skills as an observer. Pay attention to your own life, and look at what goes on around you. Decide what is important, and what you can do to build on that to make your life better. Reject denial and refuse to be abused. Enable the blessings in your life, and protect your freedoms.

CHAPTER 5

DECENCY vs. RUDENESS

Recipe for Destruction

The recipe for a great burger is pretty simple. Shape up a handful of meat, season to taste, cook on a hot grill, insert into bun, dress it all up, and voila. Grilled veggies are easy too. A recipe is a well-organized plan based on chemistry. Just follow directions and that pie crust won't end up becoming your dog's new Frisbee. Not so, the recipe for a good family. Creating a healthy family is more like preparing a complicated menu, with appetizers, entrees, side dishes, beverages and desserts.

Everyone who has baked a cake or been part of a family knows they are not fool proof. To err is unfailingly human. Trouble is, there are no two families alike, and no one-size-fits-all recipes that lay out the way to become healthy, happy clans. Ingredients go bad. Sometimes the chemistry in a family does too. Much to our dismay, catastrophe and bad blood are uninvited but inevitable guests at every table and in every family. Just like any formula for success, healthy food and solid families are products of time, love, and attention. Perseverance and hard work might produce a sound family, but there is no assurance. Outside forces over which we have no control impact parents, families, children, and culture. The human family is vulnerable.

Although most of our food sources are monitored and safe through government inspections and laws, accidents happen. Anyone who has suffered food poisoning understands the pain and distress caused by toxic bugs that get into our gut. From E. coli to Salmonella, ingestion of dangerous microbes can lead to severe discomfort at best, and a horrible death at worst. Fortunately, most of us survive occasional bouts of food poisoning to feast again; albeit, a bit more cautiously. But horrible doesn't begin to describe what happens to adults and children living in violent families. There is no antidote for this poison.

There are plenty of food police telling us what we can and cannot eat. Yet bad conduct and incidents of relationship abuse too often go unnoticed, unreported, and un- or under prosecuted. Only when violence is public do we pay attention. Even then, unless it has star or shock quality, it will only be sensationalized briefly in the media before fading away. Most people have little understanding of the effect of domestic violence on society. But our culture is an organic body of evidence that shows us who we are. What we see is an angry culture in distress.

Real stories of violence are ugly. Too ugly. Even the media admits that fact. It was their reason for leaving the press galley vacant throughout the gruesome trial of the Pennsylvania abortionist convicted of murder. His story was a reality show most didn't want to see, and didn't want others to see. The case was so abhorrent it was reduced to minimal coverage. The trial was a tale of family violence. The worst kind of family violence: feticide, infanticide, and murder. It was an illustration of the many forms violence takes, and how relationship violence becomes societal violence. The termination of life must be seen for what it is: an act of violence. There is no dignity in killing. When it is against the innocent, it is sacrilege. Public opinion should determine what is newsworthy. Journalists do not speak for the millions of Americans who want the truth instead of spun yarn.

Media have the right to report whatever they choose, regardless of how biased it may be. But we have the right to decide what to believe.

Faulty ingredients produce a toxic family the same way a mad-cow burger or a feces-contaminated salad produces life-threatening disease. Not all burgers or salads are bad, it's only the infected ones that we have to worry about. Like contaminated foods that show no visible signs of peril, a sick family or individual is capable of blending unnoticed into its surroundings. The nature of violence is subterranean; it only surfaces to do its dastardly deeds. It is a snake so meticulously camouflaged in its cryptic skin you don't see it until after you've been bitten. Violence, abuse and terrorism can hide undetected just below the radar until ready to strike. According to herpetologists, for every snake we see, there are a dozen more we didn't. It is an unsettling but symbolic fact of life we can relate to. As we see more and more violence in America we can only imagine what is to come.

Violent people, like snakes, are unrepentant creatures that intentionally lash out at their victims. Whether they reside in our homes or on our streets, it is time to get the hoses and flush them out of their holes. When we bring violent people into the light, they can be identified and held accountable. But to do so requires the willingness to look beyond their camouflage and see them for who they are, wherever they are. That is our national challenge: to get out of our comfort zones and reject them. Violence in all forms is destroying our culture national treasure: the family. We have to be as intentional in punishing violence as the violent are in punishing us.

A ROSE BY ANY OTHER NAME

America owns the *Constitution*, and its eloquence distinguishes us from every other country in the world. Our exceptionalism as a nation was born and bred on the values and principles contained in that uniquely American document. It is what draws immigrants to our shores. Every soul here came from somewhere else, including the earliest inhabitants. The United States welcomes people from all over the world. As a result, we have enormous conflict over the principles and values we are all supposed to abide by.

The Constitution and Rule of Law provide concrete guidelines for acceptable behavior. But in order to be effective, they have to be enforced. That is proving to be very difficult in a culture suffused with conflicting notions of right and wrong. Flocks of legal eagles challenge laws in court in the name of diversity and tolerance. As a result, American standards of morality and justice are being dismantled, not reaffirmed. Perhaps in the mayhem and naiveté of our youth as a new nation we are in denial. There are people who have no desire to melt into the pot that is America and live under the *Constitution*. Some would rather steal the pot. Not to embrace America, but to kill her. If you don't like stew, you're not going to eat it. And we are, indeed, a veritable stew.

Every culture has rules and norms that define the behaviors generally considered acceptable. We are never going to agree. Concepts of decency and rudeness are perceived differently by different people, and under different circumstances. A secluded membership resort for visitors wanting to get away from it all, including their clothes, requires guests to bare all. In the private world of a nudist colony, it is deemed rude to be clothed. Down the road at a world-renowned luxury golf resort, the police will be called to haul you away if you turn up on the greens in your birthday suit. A loud-mouthed drunk will be a problem at a school PTA meeting, and a welcomed customer at the local watering hole. Decent may be a concept in the eyes of the beholder, but laws are created to protect the rights of all.

Rudeness is considered offensive and irritating, while decency refers to a higher moral standard. Personal, social, and legal prohibitions define our ideas of decency. They set the bar for what we can and cannot do without getting into trouble or feeling embarrassed. A decent person is usually seen as an individual of good character. To earn a decent living suggests a good income. Therefore, if decent implies good, then *in*decent must not be good.

Public indecency is a reflection of the wider swath of social deterioration that is unfolding in communities everywhere. The exposure of private body parts in public is called Indecent Exposure. It will land you an arrest and the label "Sex Offender". Because there are several levels under the label, it can also be the sobering consequence of being arrested for urinating in public. Exposure is considered *indecent*, and the act illegal, whether or not it was intended as a sexual act. It is about personal and social responsibility. Cultures lacking public restrooms or indoor plumbing may not consider answering the 'call of nature' on the street offensive or indecency. It is an unnecessary and irresponsible act in a civilized country with plenty of public facilities.

Despite the tolerance and sympathy permeating much of our legal system, sex offenders are still seen by most people as social outcasts. It is a population few want to be associated with or live next door to. Most cities post crime maps on the internet showing the locations and profiles of sex offenders. The maps are easily accessible for public viewing and are an invaluable resource for information about local crimes. Warning! It may be disturbing to discover who you neighbor is. Police departments also distribute flyers to residents when certain sex offenders move into a neighborhood. Flyers carry a statement reminding people that public awareness is the best way to promote safety.

Awareness is critical to public health and safety. Sex offenses are acts of violation based on the need for power and control. They are not based on sexual desire. Sex is merely the instrument used in the commission of sexual violence. Sentencing of sex offenders often depends on the skill of defense attorneys and the leniency of judges. Many heinous acts by depraved people go under-punished and are repeated.

America witnessed numerous examples of public indecency in the demonstrations around the country called "Occupy Wall Street". Calling the mayhem in these venues "in-decent" doesn't capture the full essence of behavior exhibited. In some encampments, indecent behavior was elevated to the level of *obscenity*. Defecations on squad cars, public sex, rape, violence, drug abuse, trespass and criminal damage flowed like sludge. City after city reverberated in well-organized and well-funded chaos. Americans watched in disgust as coverage of the out of control throngs filled the evening news.

Protest is an American freedom. Violence, anarchy, and crime are not. The Occupy movement was heralded by some special interest groups, government officials and media as a great American expression of collective dissent and revolution. Few spoke of the violence, casualties, and millions of dollars occupiers cost businesses and taxpayers. To supporters, the protest was a good, politically correct thing to do no matter what the cost. Acceptance of such aggression and lawlessness demonstrates how divided we are as a country and the direction we are headed in. Tolerance and support of violence as a means of protest signifies the end of civil society. It showed America and the world that we are a culture in decline.

RANK AND FILE

Believing the ends justify the means in fighting for one's causes is a corruption of the idea of civilization. *Occupy* gives a stupefying peak at the level of decadence that occupies our culture. Dissent that utilizes violence, obscenity, and crime is mobocracy; mob rule, not democracy. Freedom of speech is not freedom to destroy. Violent revolution is the moniker of oppressed and illiterate people in undeveloped autocracies around the world. America is a country with elected representation and venues for discussion. When personal beliefs become public activism that condones criminal behavior and violence, a free society is jeopardized. When it is cheered on and tolerated we have slipped into treacherous water. Where did so much hate and social malignancy come from? It is a question that begs consideration if we want to stop it. The first and greatest classroom is the family. If we don't like the graduates, it's because we have failed as teachers. Someone raises the children who become the abusers and criminals in society. The recipe we've been using is missing a few ingredients. Those ingredients are accountability and responsibility.

In previous generations there was general agreement throughout the United States regarding what is considered acceptable behavior and language. Children were taught manners and responsibility by parents, teachers, and communities, as well as the family traditions of faith and culture. Regardless of their ethnicity, politics, or religious beliefs, families shared responsibility for the privilege of American citizenship. Most people endeavored to hold themselves and their children accountable to that privilege as they lived their lives. *That has changed.*

During a soccer game in Utah, a volunteer referee made a call a seventeen year old goalie didn't like. In another time, before swearing and screaming on tennis courts was allowed, and parents physically fighting over Little League and youth football games was common, sports were safe for kids and game officials. In this incident, the referee made the call and the goalie went after him. The player angrily punched the man in the head. Reeling, dizzy, and bleeding, the referee was rushed to the emergency room, where he went into a coma. He was a beloved family man and friend who died because of a call he made in a high school soccer game. That should curdle the blood of America. Absent good sportsmanship, respect, and common decency, sporting events become just another arena for violence.

A cry for 'civility' is a really a demand for special treatment. It is an attempt to intimidate others with guilt in order to get something. Like 'transparency', it is an overused word that has no meaning because there is no honesty behind it. Basic concepts of personal and social responsibility no longer exist. Some of the loudest voices for civility are themselves the biggest offenders of civil rights and freedoms. An example is the increasing effort to censor free speech by banning certain words from common usage. When the word 'bossy' is determined to be sexist, demeaning and unacceptable, we are in trouble as a culture. Demanding obedience to a narrow version of freedom is incompatible with the true meaning of civil liberty. Professing transparency while tapping phones is not transparency, it is deception. It is hypocrisy to claim to have moral standards when those standards only apply to everyone else. It is any wonder so many American youth are angry, rude, and disrespectful?

Student on teacher assault is on the increase in public schools. Many teachers have classrooms that are out of control and dangerous, especially in inner city schools. Some are forced to take aggressive action in self-defense against students who threaten and use violence on them. Not every school has strict policies for dealing with bad behavior. Some kids get away with violence and abuse with little or no consequence. At worst, an aggressive student may be transferred to another school or class. There is no consistency in dealing with bad behavior in public schools.

The U.S. Department of Education released results of a survey that looks at punishment of school children. In 96,000 public schools surveyed, 49,000,000 children were expelled for bad behavior. Results showed that minorities and inner-city children in lower grades were most affected.[1] The high numbers of expulsions in those groups are blamed on lack of opportunity, race, and social disadvantage. The survey is a case of 'blaming the victim'. Its teachers and schools that are acting badly, not the armies of juvenile troublemakers.

What is unfortunate is the proposed correction of this imbalance. Rather than removing problem children from school, more *tolerance* is recommended. Citing unfair disadvantages of race, economic status, and location, children are to remain in school and receive counseling. Disruption in the classroom and risk to other students and faculty is apparently not a primary concern. Instead of giving out-of-control children the discipline and structure they need, we will give them special treatment *because* of their bad behavior. Acting out in school is a cry for help. It is a screaming '9-1-1' begging society to respond. Answering the call with excuses and tolerance ignores the emergency. Coddling bad behavior teaches children how to work the system and the adults who run it. It neglects individual responsibility by accusing schools of unfair discrimination.

According to the survey, there is a positive correlation between problem behaviors in minor children and the high percentage of minorities in prison. The correlation implied is racism. It is an unfounded assumption. Based on the results of this survey, the Attorney General calls for more tolerance and less punishment of juvenile offenders. More tolerance, less discipline, and counseling are not going to motivate angry, disenfranchised children to change aggressive behavior. Removing student expulsion as a consequence and replacing it with therapy fails to teach accountability. It also removes the burden of responsibility from parents, who are the biggest part of the equation. This is what we need to understand: the stream of criminals from minority and poor populations will continue until society changes its attitudes about them, and they change their attitudes about society.

Viewing punishment as abuse instead of the logical outcome for bad behavior teaches disrespect, not principles. Many of the children in the survey are being raised in a violent culture. That doesn't make kids wise, it makes them street-smart. And savvy kids know when they have the upper hand in a situation. Violence teaches kids how to get power and control. This is how we create future serpents in the house and in society. Prison is just the end game. History repeats itself. We have to reinforce the benefits of good behavior by attaching clear consequences for bad behavior. When children don't learn healthy behavior at home or at school, where will they learn it?

In the survey, there is no evidence that thousands of teachers are bigoted racists who single-out minority children to expel. Classroom violence is a direct consequence of the breakdown of the family and social order. Crime is a choice, regardless of race, opportunity, or economic status. At the same time, racism may be a trigger for the high percentage of crimes committed against *non*-minorities.[2] When the mentality of victimization, unfairness, and entitlement is promoted, there will be retaliation. Excusing behavioral problems in children by labeling them victims of social injustice is itself social injustice. It is *identity politics,* and wrongly advances the belief that race, social class, and disadvantage *make* and *keep* people victims. Instead of promoting dignity and self-respect, it undermines the spirit by fostering anger and resentment.

The incidence of teacher-student sexual liaisons is also an increasing problem in schools. Social media and networking have made outside personal relationships between teachers and students not only possible, but common. When educators seek to make students friends and social interests, such interactions exceed the propriety of the teacher-student relationship. It is a conflict of professional ethics and contributes to the blurring of appropriate boundaries for both. Teachers used to be expected to be exemplary role models for students, and students were expected to show respect for their teachers. That ideal has been corrupted both ways, with not much being done to stop it.

Bullying on campuses, school buses, cell phones and the internet has escalated. Parents have great concern for the safety of their children. Common decency and empathy do not exist in the worst of these situations. Videos taken by students watching as kids are being beaten up and abused show onlookers cheering, laughing, and failing to intervene as children and monitors are abused and beaten up. But bullying goes both ways. It is not just students who are the bullies. Children report incidents where teachers attack and belittle them for the clothes they wear or the food in their lunchboxes. Some students have even been given bad grades for disagreeing with their teacher's political views.

The demise of structure and discipline in the classroom, and a popular culture of rudeness and disrespect have produced high dropout rates and low test scores in high school students. In a youth-driven culture that thrives on entitlement and irresponsibility, we are losing students and academic achievement as test scores drop compared to other countries. Despite the fact that the United States spends more on education than any other country, our kids consistently produce test scores in science and math that are way below those of Korea, Singapore, China and many other countries.[3]

We have become a country that worries more about what's in a kid's lunchbox, how much he or she weighs, and whether a six year old is getting politically correct sex education than the ability of our children to think, read, write or find their own state on a map. The more money we spend, the stupider our children are becoming in the new age school model. Just like the pledge of allegiance and the American flag, manners, decency and morality are disappearing from classrooms. Most children learn more from games, music, movies, social media and friends than they do in school or at home. In a hip climate, being rude is cool. And cool is everything. With so many problems in so many schools, it is no wonder home schooling has become the option of choice for many Americans. Parents looking to have more control over the content of their children's education as well as their safety are seeking other alternatives to public school, and the results are remarkable.

FOSSILS AND CROCODILES

Placing dashboard cameras on police cars has been a brilliant way of recording the interactions between law enforcement and civilians during police stops. The cams produce an evidentiary visual and audio narrative that validates reports by officers and the statements of those stopped. On a dark night in Georgia, a popular young actress significantly under the influence of alcohol found herself cuffed and charged for judicial interference when her husband was arrested for a DUI. Dash cam footage is public information, and the recording of the incident quickly went viral on the internet.

What emerged were indignations and assertions that she could say and do anything she wanted because she was an American, standing on American soil. That being a true statement, she soon found out that she was also going to be held responsible for breaking the law, as an American who can say and do anything she wants. Furthermore, there was an implication made by the actress that her name and fame should mean something, i.e., entitlement or special consideration of some kind.

After being charged, spending time in jail, and paying a fine, the lady was released. Cameras flashing and tapes rolling, she promptly made a public apology to the police, and to her adoring audience. In postscript to the drunk driving event she was a party to, and pre-script to her new soon to be released movie, the actress made a sad commentary. *She said she did not remember saying the things she did,* and, that she should have stayed in her car as she was told to do by the officer.

Not remembering what we say or do while intoxicated is a blackout, a dangerous medical condition. Not being able to control what we say and do is disinhibition. While also a potentially dangerous state of mind, to lose ones inhibitions is to have those less than charming thoughts, feelings and actions we usually hold in check run amok. Sometimes they come back to bite us. Entitlement is a sorry belief to hold on to, as is disrespectful behavior. Although a sense of entitlement and privilege are a common domain of entertainers and elitists of all genres, it is seen as arrogant and egotistical by regular people. But in a culture that accepts rudeness and arrogance, being bad is better than being good.

Common decency is analogous to common sense, if you think about it. Common sense, according to Merriam-Webster, is "sound and prudent judgment based on a simple perception of the situation or facts," and by Cambridge dictionary as "the basic level of practical knowledge and judgment that we all need to help us live in a reasonable and safe way". There is comfort in those eleven familiar words: sound, prudent, judgment, simple perception, facts, and, basic, practical, knowledge, reasonable, and safe. When we use common sense, we are in a state of decency, because our inherent humanity is based on all of those common English words.

The hot word in our national lexicon today is sustainability. It is popularly used as a motivation for change in our basic way of life. The term usually refers to all things green, but it is an important concept to consider for the critical issues we face right now as a culture. Just like fossils, fuel, and crocodiles, the ability to *sustain* is a question of endurance and the ability to withstand over the long haul. If our relationships, businesses, governments, and culture followed the premises of common sense, we might be able to increase the sustainability of the most important of our natural resources: our families, our dreams, and our country. In order to commit the time and energy required to sustain something, to preserve it, we have to have a strong desire to do so. With the country in crises on so many levels, the majority of Americans polled do not believe that we are in a place we even want to sustain. Across the country, people want change, but not what we are morphing into.

Diversity and multi-culturalism are the retaining walls of our country's immigrant foundation, and united we are strong. A divided nation is not sustainable. In the Civil Rights movement of the 1960's, the whole point of integration was to abolish segregation and affirm equality so that we might stand the tests of time shoulder to shoulder with our fellow Americans.[4] In the truest sense of the word, integration was a joining, a coming together. It didn't abolish our many diverse cultures and peoples, rather, it enabled all of us to be blended into the common mix called America. Today we are in an era of dis-integration, and it looks an awful lot like segregation again.

SHIFTING SHAPES

Violence finds safe harbor in many circumstances, and hidden in the faces of many people. Only the most perceptive are able to recognize the presence of a clever monster. It is easy to be deceived. When people have been numbed or frightened by abuse, they may not be able react to the subtle warning signs of danger, even when it's staring them in the face. Dangerous characters are not always easy to identify. They may merely be seen as weird or unpleasant. We will have to become better observers.

Nobody in Boston saw the evil that quietly lurked among the cheering spectators at the finish line of the sunny, April 15th 2013 Patriot's Day Marathon. Nonetheless, it was there. With cunning brutality, the murderers stalked the crowded sidewalks, stopping only briefly to place their bomb-filled backpacks. Then, with a well-planned strategy, they departed, as easily as they had arrived, to witness from afar the explosions that would desiccate the lives, bodies, and dreams of hundreds of innocent people.

Only after the death of one, and the capture of the second alleged bomber did Boston and America become acquainted with the sophisticated preparation and plans that were to become such horrific acts of terrorism, and the faces of death that were behind them. Classmates, friends, coaches and team mates were deceived by the two men they thought they knew. They were shocked to realize what they had done. But the men had a long and sordid history of both domestic violence and social violence. From their earliest childhoods to the lethal end of their terrorist acts, violence was in their blood. They had slipped through many cracks on the way to the Marathon, including the FBI, who had been warned about them by Russian officials.

Utter shock and sheer joy rippled simultaneously through a Cleveland, Ohio, neighborhood. Three missing women and a six-year old child were discovered and rescued from the horror chambers that had been their home for almost a decade. As teenagers, the two girls and another young woman had been kidnapped off the street in broad daylight. They were held hostage by a well-known and longtime resident of the area.

The child was born to one of the girls as a result of rape midway through her imprisonment. Other pregnancies over the years had allegedly been terminated as a result of brutal beatings by the rapist. Incredibly, nobody knew the awfulness that was in their midst. None of the victims had been seen or heard as they suffered at the hands of their captor and torturer. Ariel Castro was a violent husband who took his violence to the street in order to capture victims against whom he could continue to perpetuate heinous acts of domestic violence.

No one suspected anything unusual of the man who drove a school bus. Even though windows on his house were boarded up, and friends reportedly had never seen the inside rooms of his home. The admitted kidnapper passed for an average kind of guy. He just fit in, getting along well with neighbors, and even being friends with the father of one of the girls he held hostage. But police records showed there had been several domestic violence assault charges made against the man. On several occasions he allegedly inflicted such severe injuries on his former wife she had to be hospitalized. When the victim, Castro, attorneys, and law enforcement failed to show up for court, the case was dropped and he went free. His ex-wife later died.

Castro had a very long history of violence. Yet, allegedly, there was no follow up on reports and phone calls made to police by worried neighbors claiming to witness bizarre activities on his property. Whether it was apathy or lax protocol on the part of law enforcement and others in a position to suspect something was wrong with this man we will never know. What is clear, was his pattern of behavior with women, and his pathological need for power and control. Violence was the means to that ends. Ariel Castro was a perpetrator of horrific domestic violence. But in private and in public, he was undetected and unchallenged. Only after capture was his true nature revealed. Castro was not what he pretended to be as he went about his daily life. *He was a monster.* Once convicted and sentenced to life in prison, Castro committed suicide. It is a common response by sociopaths when their ability to commit further acts of violence is terminated.

A pleasant, well-kept home in a quiet Phoenix community suddenly turned into the grisly death scene of a young man. He was shot twice and stabbed almost thirty times. The man's throat was slit from ear to ear so violently he was virtually decapitated. In the privacy of the couple's twisted and toxic relationship, the man was murdered in cold blood by his girlfriend of two years. She was arrested, tried, and found guilty of pre-meditated first-degree murder. The violence was a particularly heinous act of domestic violence. The murder contaminated the lives of neighbors, family and friends. And the jury and courtroom were traumatized by shocking photos, testimony and evidence over the course of the trial. Domestic violence is a crime against all of society.

It took four years from her arrest to get the conviction. By the time the killer came to trial, what once was the smiling face of an attractive young woman was contorted and dark. She bore the icy smirk of a calculating assassin. Although friends and associates testified to her attributes and shortcomings, the term *killer* had not been one of them. At least, not until she admitted to murdering her lover. The woman was not liked, not warm, not kind; but she had hidden the depth of evil in her soul extremely well. Everyone had been fooled, including the unfortunate victim.

Violence finds safe harbor in many places, and in many types of people. Only the most perceptive recognize the presence of a clever monster. They are easily mistaken as 'strange' or 'weird' and avoided. But sociopaths specialize in hiding secrets. Even mental health professionals can be deceived. Unfortunately, only those willing to see are even looking; the rest often settle for the naiveté of ignorance or denial. Abused people are often too numbed and frightened to react to signs of violence when it's staring them in the face. Trauma has the ability to paralyze normal self-defense mechanisms. The inability to react to danger is a tragic by-product of violence. In a perfect world, every human would be equipped with keen awareness and the ability to protect themselves. But in the real world, millions of crime victims go through life too wounded to recognize menace. Domestic and societal violence enforce silence in their victims. Violent crime feeds on the vulnerability of individuals and society. The antidote is reduction of that vulnerability.

No laws or agencies exist through which families may be inspected to assure that they are violence-free. Unless a police or welfare report is filed, 911 is called, or a crime is committed, no one is going to have access to a private home. We just don't know what goes on behind the closed doors of a household until something happens. Each of us has an obligation to be alert to the symptoms of distress and anger in ourselves and others. Awareness of surroundings and behavior is critical, but to be aware requires that we are conscious. Consciousness is the best defense against abuse. By putting voice to our consciousness, we break the silence that keeps us at risk.

"If You See Something, Say Something," is a slogan created and licensed for use by The U.S. Department of Homeland Security in 2010. It is a government campaign to raise public awareness of signs of terrorism and crime. Millions of dollars in federal grants have been awarded to spread the campaign across the U.S.A. A Gallup Poll found that most Americans (55%) had never heard of the campaign or slogan.[5] Pollsters also discovered that few understood the slogan referred to reporting suspected terrorism and crime.

In Eastern states, 64% of residents were likely to recognize the phrase, compared to 37% in the West. Results of the poll suggest differences in awareness between regions might be due to the fact that more terrorist acts and attempts have taken place in the East. But the largest differences exist between education levels. Of those without college degrees, only 41% were likely to recognize the slogan, compared with 55% of those with degrees. The greatest difference was between high school graduates (35%), and people with postgraduate degrees (57%).

The poll underscores the absence of awareness in the country regarding crime. Although education is a critical resource for bringing awareness to the public, it cannot make people aware. Experience is awareness. We can learn something academically, but we may not understand it. Based on the poll, on average 47% of Americans, less than one out of two, are aware enough to 'say something' if they see suspicious behavior. Not good enough to help prevent violence.

FREEDOM IS AS FREEDOM DOES

In a free society, liberty comes with both positive and negative consequences. The polarization of America has triggered emotions and confusion reminiscent of our founding as a nation. We are angry and disillusioned by a Government we don't trust, an economy that is breaking us, and a culture in decline. Once upon a time our lives were happier, and our streets were safer. Pockets of peaceful Hometown, USA, still exist, but are no longer shielded from the problems of crime and violence. It's time to set our differences aside and define the common ground our families and country stand together on.

America knows how to pull together as a nation. Thomas Paine wrote his epic pamphlet, Common Sense,[8] during the pre-Revolutionary War era of Colonial America. He eloquently argued in support of Separatism from England, and American Patriotism. Independence, equal representation of the people and her colonies, and the monarchy-free country we now live in evolved partly because of his common sense ideas and reason. He had a vision and a plan, and together, they became a nation. It wasn't easy, but it was simple. Most people are responsible bearers of the rights and privileges colonial armies fought to establish. But there will always be others who usurp the rights of others for their own benefit. It is our turn to protect the rights, families, and country we share from those who mean us harm. It is time to put our house in order as if our lives depended on it. They do!

What you can do: Using common sense and common decency as templates, do what we know best: refuse to surrender to tyranny. The threat of violence is everywhere. Through cooperation and direction we can craft a plan of action to strengthen our values, reject moral decline, and take back our country. Success doesn't require millions of dollars and failed campaigns to develop a nation of conscious citizens. It takes millions of *conscious people* uniting to protect the honor, integrity and safety of the nation. National health begins in the family, and family health is the foundation of the nation.

CHAPTER 6

PERSONAL and SOCIAL RESPONSIBILITY

"We drove away from the house in a black hearse. Heavy velvet curtains were draped across the windows, so I couldn't see out. It was very late, and I was tired because they had forced me to stay awake for the ceremony. All I wanted to do was go to sleep, but I was sitting on my uncle's lap, and… he….he kept waking me back up." Collette was beginning to stutter as she stared vacantly through the glass doors behind me.

"On…on…on the long pedestal… in front… of me… was, was a…." she gripped the arms of the chair, struggling to speak: "It was a small…… *casket*……a little, small casket," she whispered, dropping her head in momentary silence. "Not like the big ones daddy usually put in the back of the limousine. And…..it was pink," she stammered, "and it scared me. It terrified me!" The woman gasped. Her shoulders hunched over and her eyes flew open as if she had suddenly seen a ghost. I was about to discover that the vision before her was worse than a ghost. Much worse.

"What frightened you about that small, pink casket, Collette?" I inquired softly. An emotional chasm opened up between us as she looked away and clenched her jaw. "Was this a funeral for a little girl?" She took a deep breath. "Collette, can you tell me about that night?" I pressed. It had taken us many months to get to this point in her therapy. There was a possibility she would shut down as she had done before, unable to bear witness to her pain.

In the late 1980's and early 1990's there was a sudden increase in the number of animal mutilations being reported, mostly in Western states. Simultaneously, the practice of Satanism reared its ugly head around the country. Initially, as evidence of violence against humans related to the occult began turning up, the country was stunned. Ghoulish rites and practices were sensationalized in tabloids. Photos and sordid details allegedly sneaked out of Black Masses splashed across the news. Some people laughed: witches and warlocks? But others *shuddered.*

Reports in the media triggered copycat crimes and false narratives. Deeply disturbed people seeking notoriety came out in droves telling detailed stories about their own abuse by Satanists. Most proved to be unfounded. Unfortunately, these fraudulent testimonials began to negate the legitimacy of real cases. America didn't want to believe any of it. Such unconscionable tales of torture and violence were the products of Hollywood movies or the fantasies of deranged minds, not real life. Once uncovered, however, the undeniable facts spoke for themselves. There were too many victims. Ritual abuse could not be denied.[1] Enforcement agencies around the country soon realized the level of deviancy they were up against. Specialized task forces assembled to locate and apprehend those engaged in the criminal practices of Satanism. Officers combed through the darkness of night searching for these predators and their victims. Some were found, most were not.

The Mortuary of Eternal Rest was a third generation family-owned business. It occupied a four-story Victorian house that served as county funeral parlor as well as Collette's home. She was terrified by what she heard from the bowels of the old mansion. "But mostly," she began, "I hated the awful stench that came up through the vents when I knew daddy and uncle were downstairs working." Her chin dropped to her chest. After a few moments she looked up at me. "I had to eat all my meals in the kitchen. It was just above the embalming chambers." She shook her head slowly from side to side. "Only the sweet smell of flowers that always filled the viewing rooms kept me from vomiting. If I threw up, they made me eat it again."

She coughed, but it was more like gagging, as she removed her glasses to blow her nose: "On Saturday nights....That's when everything changed." The air between us was heavy as the pale woman tilted her head and looked directly into my eyes: "That's when bad things happened......bad, bad things happened late at night." We both sat motionless. Collette's stare was ice-cold. "It was that Saturday night when I saw what they did to Jennie." I was gripped by nausea, fearing what was next. "It was Jenni *my friend Jennie was.in the casket.* The-little-pink-casket carried Jennie."

My client Collette (my name for her) was fifty years old and beginning to process the agony of her childhood as the daughter of practicing Satanists. Collette, *Letty* as they called her, had witnessed and been the victim of some of the most heinous acts of abuse conceivable. Drugged by her own parents, Letty had been made to witness the assault and sexual violation of her best friend, Jennie, during the ritualistic sacrifice that culminated in the slitting of her throat. When her blood was drained from her tiny body into an ornate silver cup, the chalice was passed around for everyone to drink in honor of the Prince of Death. The trauma of that night remained hidden in her subconscious for decades.

The small mountain town where Letty was born was inhabited by members of her family. They were all Satanists. Isolated and sworn in blood to secrecy, the family maintained the rites and monstrosities of the cult without intrusion. Outsiders avoided contact with the clan who were perceived as odd and dangerously territorial. Except for the funerals and burials that brought them to the village for a few hours, nobody dared step foot on the dreary streets. Lost travelers, runaways and hunters who unfortunately found their way there never left. A constant supply of bodies came to the mortuary. Corpses, live humans, and animals provided a sadistic mix of victims for the rituals of Letty's town.

Collette was addicted to multiple substances by age six. She escaped from home in her early teens, but the traumas locked deep in her soul continued to torment her. There were suicide attempts. At age 27, Letty was arrested and incarcerated for trying to kill her husband, and diagnosed with severe bi-polar disorder. When she was released from prison, she stopped taking her medications and was re-arrested for assault and the attempted murder of a female neighbor. Both of Letty's adult sons were incarcerated for violent crimes. Mentally ill and alone in the world, my client faced a bleak and painful future unless she could break the shackles of her past. Her story is an extreme example of how domestic violence becomes societal violence Ritual abuse is a side of life we don't want to know or believe. It defies comprehension, but illustrates the psychosis of violence.

An eye for an eye; live by the sword, die by the sword; and, *the sins of the father:* there are many edicts that have been handed down through history to rationalize vengeance and retribution. The terms personal and social responsibility mean different things to different people. But it is mistaken to believe they are separate issues. Israel, a nation continuously at risk of terrorism, understands that murderers have the same profile before committing murder as they do after.[2] This is not rocket science. It is the science of *predictive profiling*, and has protected Israelis from hundreds of acts of terrorism. Although many Americans may not condone the technique, the nation of Israel supports the belief that *individuals and society together are responsible for the security of the country.*

In the United States, on the other hand, there is intense disagreement over personal and social responsibility. In the past few years, our national understanding of liberty and freedom seems to have gotten confused with *rights*. A sub-culture of personal and social privilege has evolved. Americans are bitterly disunited over what constitutes a "fair share" on the field of dreams of America. The argument over who is responsible for one's own existence seems irreconcilable. The dependent life of a damaged adult like Collette is not the same as the dependent life of an adult who chooses to be a taker.

Beyond the natural and moral imperative to look after those unable to care for themselves, good people disagree on who and what should be entitled to government gifts. Civil rights advocates insist that all men created equal is not only the manifest for equal opportunity, but for equal outcomes as well. Although well-intentioned, the outcomes piece of that pie is not an assurance of equality. In fact it is a form of social abuse. Holding out false promises that can never be fulfilled is intentional cruelty. Dishonesty does not produce positive outcomes. It violates trust, respect and decency. And those elements trigger anger.

By equating the intrinsic dignity of a human *being* with the external condition of the human *having,* we lose sight of the power of individuality and self-determination. Individual responsibility was once called self-reliance. It has been devalued in favor of the concept of entitlement. Disability claims, nutrition assistance, and unemployment are high. In a country once respected for its strong work ethic, societal stress is mounting, self-esteem is declining, and responsibility for many is a thing of past. In our hurry to level the field, we are setting people up for failure and removing the gift of personal achievement. Shirking responsibility and accountability in the name of justice is acceptable. Self-determination is replaced by redistribution of other people's assets as the path to happiness.

Competition, personal fulfillment and prosperity are not part of this system of sameness. One is not allowed to be faster, smarter, richer or prettier than another. That would be unfair. Self-reliant, independent go-getters are not valued today in the one size fits all curriculum of mass uniformity. Aggressively enforced conformity defeats uniqueness and the potential present in every human being. If we are all the same, all minimized versions of some norm, who is responsible? Which one of us will be held accountable in such dummied down circumstances?

There is a clever car commercial that shows robotized well-dressed look-alike males moving along an assembly line as they receive appointments and verbal instructions from a presumed Imperial leader. When a set of keys is suddenly given to one of them by a sympathetic worker, he jumps the conveyor belt, escaping to freedom in the luxury car waiting for him just outside the plant. With Imperial TIE fighters in hot pursuit, he smiles into the rear- view mirror and blasts away, a liberated man. When our guy goes for it, we cheer. It is our in nature to be free and pursue our dreams, not drones in the beehive.

Utter the word accountability, and the response from most people is usually a blank stare. When asked what the words responsibility and accountability mean, few are able to define them. We use both interchangeably, not realizing their subtle differences. Although they are not the same, the words share an important commonality: *trustworthiness* - how dependable we are.

To be trustworthy denotes honor and integrity. It defines who we are individually and how we conduct ourselves socially. It is character. If we are trustworthy, we will have no problem taking ownership of our own behavior, no matter how painful or embarrassing it may be. In fact, we must. That is the mark of a principled man or woman. And it is one of the most important character traits we can instill in children.

Because trustworthiness is intentional, it requires a conscious decision that must be made consistently under different circumstances, and that requires commitment and practice. Over a lifetime, our level of trustworthiness will be put to the test many times. It is not that we strive to be perfect, but that we endeavor as best we can to be our better selves. Reliability and dependability reflects the highest good in our hearts and extends outward to others. Not everyone is capable of heeding the challenge, however. It important for those who are able and willing to set a higher moral standard for ourselves and one another.

To be ethical and principled is to be very uncool today. It is dangerous to your health. Being a legitimate good guy might get you bullied by those who enjoy the power of being bad. Social indecency has replaced the principles of good character we have traditionally revered. From pre-school to college, conception to death, Americans of all ages are being subjected to a transformation of values. We are afraid of being attacked by an angry individual or group for speaking our minds. As a culture, Americans are being forced to drink from a dirty swamp. What

ROLE MODELS AND SUPER-HEROES

There is increasingly less common ground on which Americans can agree when it comes to the issue of responsibility. With one exception, however: paying taxes. Under the control of the Internal Revenue Service, all of us are held to a system of taxation and collection so notoriously abusive that we share a common dread in just seeing the letters IRS. Once under audit or interrogation by the little house of horrors, a.k.a., the IRS, we are all assumed guilty until proven innocent, the exact opposite of the rule of law where we are presumed innocent and must be proved guilty. And proving one's innocence can be a painful, expensive, and debilitating process conducted without sympathy by IRS tax attorneys. Paying taxes is the one level playing field all income earning Americans have in common.

With unlimited authority to come after us if we are delinquent in filing annual returns or paying our taxes, over 90,000 agents from the agency are empowered to seize, levy, and take property and bank accounts-without notice or warrant. It is a government culture that lends itself easily to corruption and abuse. Always has been. These are not our heroes or super-heroes. They are agents of a troubled culture. The IRS has managed slip by abusing taxpayers for a long time, but we now see the agency at its worst. Illegal practices unleashed by the

IRS over the past few years targeted ordinary Americans. As a result, freedom of speech, religion and other civil rights were effectively suppressed for alleged political purposes. Their actions are a violation of the law and our Constitution, yet they persist.

The IRS is a clear example of abuse through the use of power and control. It is societal abuse and is symptomatic of a much deeper dysfunction: tyranny. And it angers us deeply because we are helpless against such enormous abuse of power. Few are so enraged they crash an airplane into an IRS office building, however. But that is what one angry taxpayer did in Austin, Texas.[3] The pilot was a 53 year old computer engineer described as an easygoing, talented musician. His family reported he was broken because tax authorities were taking away his savings. He had a grudge against the IRS, not people. And the marriage reportedly had problems. Combined, the stress of taxation, marital trouble, and anger may have sent him into a rant that ended with suicide, death, and destruction.

Negligence, intimidation, and the inability to produce supporting documents for the expenditure of over fifty million tax payer dollars for conferences and parties has put the agency in severe trouble with the United States Congress and most Americans. Try showing up for your own tax audit without those receipts for deductions and expenses you are claiming, and see how far it gets you with the IRS. As taxpayers, we are expected to account for every penny we try to deduct. Such bad behavior and violation of the law would get you and me thrown into jail. Not so for our civil servants at the IRS. Responsibility and accountability don't seem to apply to them. When it smacks us in the face, we recognize abuse for what it is.

Thousands of new agents are about to be hired by the United States Treasury in order to identify, enforce, fine and punish people who fail to purchase health insurance under the new Affordable Care Act. Anyone not in compliance with the law will face jail time as well as fines. The privacy of personal health records, identities and information and freedom of choice are permanently forfeited in this action. America needs The Iron Man to intercede on our behalf. In order to regain our rights and independence, maybe it is time for the rest of us to jump off the conveyor belt and run for our lives too. We are going to have to be our own role models, our own super-heroes, and take action to stop the abuse.

THE BLINDED CYCLOPS

In 2012, the House of Representatives filed criminal contempt charges against the highest law enforcement officer in the country, Attorney General Eric Holder. The "top cop" of the Justice Department was held in contempt by Congress for the first time in history.[4] Justice is supposed to protect, not injure us. More and more scandals and violations of trust reveal the far-and-deep reach of government abuse. Disclosure of the data-mining of everything from texts and phone calls, to emails and personal information has shocked us. Most Americans feel violated by a power over which they have no control. *This is societal violence of another kind.* The old Soviet Union excelled in spying and snooping on their own people and the rest of the world. Russia and China still do. Welcome to the new America.

Spying, lying, and corruption are disturbing, but they show how complicated and interconnected abuse is. We are a nation united in contempt for this blanket of abuse that has spread over us like a shroud. Although abuses by trusted leaders may not leave bloody wounds or bullet holes, they injure nonetheless. Threats, intimidation, and the use of power and control victimize people in domestic relationships. Those same behaviors in society and government damage lives by destroying the integrity of the nation. The experience of abuse can't be defined by degrees of misery. That is a subjective judgment no one has the right or ability to make. Abuses people may suffer enormous anguish and fear. No form of abused can be overlooked, excused or rationalized if we intend to end the many cycles of violence that poison lives.

Whether in government, communities, or relationships, violence begets violence. It is an insidious chain reaction that strings us together like puppets, unless we break the chain. But breaking chains requires both personal *and* social responsibility, and that is where we are in trouble. Breaking cycles of violence, whether domestic or societal, requires positive role models and enforcement. When enforcement is corrupt, who is responsible becomes a difficult question to answer. Our hands are tied by conflicting ideologies regarding rights, responsibilities, and personal freedoms. Unless we are willing to recognize abuse where it originates and agree on action to contain it, deterrence and reduction of violence is impossible.

If we don't believe in the importance of responsibility and accountability, they won't be part of our lives. And without those critical concepts, society is bound to chaos. The absence of responsibility and accountability is denial, a very seductive narcotic. Living in unreality allows deception to prevail. In the bliss of denial, we don't have to experience the inconvenience of truth. But reality happens. When a terrorist, an enraged spouse, or a deranged madman unleashes rage against us, we are thrust into that truth. And then we are stunned, searching feverishly to understand what happened. Much of America is in denial. We are unable to see beyond correctness and the fear of offending.

Ex-Navy enlistee, Aaron Alexis, shot and killed 12 people at the Navy Yard in Washington, D.C., before dying at the scene. Information on the killer revealed a history of problems with anger, domestic violence, multiple arrests, using firearms in the commission of crimes, and serious mental illness. While still in the Navy, the sailor was demoted for weapons violations. Despite these facts, his self-reported emotional disturbances and stated dislike of America, Alexis had recently been given a ten-year security clearance to work as a subcontractor at the naval installation. From the earliest moment following the shooting at the Yard, the media hustled false and biased information out to the public. Reporters tippy-toed around the land mines of incoming information about Alexis. They desperately tried to avoid the truth about the shooter. Glaring red flags were unfortunately ignored or set-aside by authorities who could have taken steps to protect Alexis and his victims.

Jared Lochner in Tucson, Adam Lanza at Sandy Hook, Christopher Dorner in Los Angeles, James Holmes in Aurora, Major Nidal Hasan at Fort Hood, the students at Columbine, and hundreds of other violent killers share a common history. They were filled with anger, participated in some form of domestic abuse, and had mental problems. Hundreds of people looked the other way or didn't want to see what these killers telegraphed long before they murdered. *Their families and society failed them, so they went, unfettered, to their terrible destinies.*

LIGHT THAT BLINDS

Day after day we hear about violent crime in America. We are inevitably shocked, as if we individually and in concert have nothing to do with it. During the Viet Nam Era, Americans for the first time in history watched war being fought *live* on T.V. When we had seen enough, we just turned it off and went to bed. Then and now, we are isolated and disconnected from the ugliness in the world as we sit in the safety of our homes. The traumas and madness are *out there*; not our problem.

Humans are very creative when attempting to avoid responsibility. Making excuses comes easy. Being made to answer for one's conduct does not. Most of us don't like getting busted. It's uncomfortable, especially if the consequences are dire. To avoid accountability, we come up with convincing excuses to dispute our guilt or negligence, even if it means lying. Although it may not be pathological, lying is a toxic way of conniving the truth. It usually backfires. For example: I might be driving the getaway car for the bank robbers, but I didn't actually participate in the robbery. So, I am accountable for my presence in the car, in fact, in the driver's seat. But I didn't go into the bank and hold up the teller. Am I equally responsible with the robbers for the crime? Unfortunately for stupid me, yes, the courts will probably charge us all as felons. A reasonable adult could have, or should have known what was going on, and chosen not to be part of the crime.

The terms accountable and responsible are neither welcome nor common in modern culture. They've been discarded as discriminatory and unjust. Holding people answerable for their conduct is often viewed as discrimination. Some people live from a deeply ingrained sense of victimization. They can't help it, it's not their fault, they insist. This is an example of the *victim mentality*. It finds its way into courts as a defense for everything from shoplifting to the commission of violent crime. In this mindset, expectation of responsibility and accountability is deemed offensive, if not unconstitutional.

Pity and sympathy go a long way in the court of the heart. But in society, enforcement of liability and prosecution of crimes is based on the law, not emotion. People once had basic agreement on the difference between right and wrong, and good and bad. That notion has been replaced with increasing tolerance for bad behavior. Society has lost its sense of culpability, and that loss foretells a crumbling culture. The future depends on our ability as a country to reclaim and reaffirm honor. Responsible behavior at home, in schools, our communities, and government shows we accept and own the condition of our lives. It is irresponsible to believe we will correct what is wrong, and protect what is right in America by tolerating less.

The framers of our Constitution set specific limits on the power of government in order to protect the rights of the individual and the separate states. In clear understanding of the dangers of despotism when power is in the hands of a few, our Founding Fathers sought to implement a system of checks and balances that would forever preserve and protect liberty. America would be a republic represented by a government elected by the people, for the people, granting power to the people, not to a few in governance. The Bill of Rights granting our individual liberties and rights is as important and at risk today as it was when that document was crafted. When America declared Independence from England, it meant we would no longer be *subjects*, but individuals with rights and liberties never before given to an entire country. In independence each of us is also held responsible for those freedoms. Independence is not to be misconstrued to mean unaccountable.

VEILS OF PERCEPTION

A culture defines itself in many ways. Movies, music, art, literature, advertisements and social media reflect our lives and what we value. But language is our vehicle of connection with each other. Through language, humans have the unique ability to articulate thoughts, emotions, desires and aspirations. So when speech is filtered through sieves of control and correctness, open expression is compromised. For example, there is an effort to eliminate use of the term "domestic violence". In New Mexico, activists call it Relationship Conflict.[5] The word 'conflict' potentially minimizes the seriousness of domestic violence. Reducing it to "dispute, squabble, or disagreement" doesn't sound so bad. Words are powerful, and the strongest must be used to define violence between humans. Using both words, "domestic" and "violence," unmistakably defines the crime.

Cosmopolitan magazine referred to domestic violence as "intimate terrorism." Yet 'intimate' may be an incorrect description of the relationship. It implies closeness and friendship. A relationship by blood, domicile, or marriage doesn't need to be intimate to be violent. It's not likely a divorced couple fighting over child support or the house are feeling intimate and friendly. Former Secretary of Homeland Security, Janet Napolitano, refused to call blowing up an airplane or subway "terrorism". With the stroke of a pen, she changed the word for acts of terrorism to *"man-caused disasters."*[6] Does that make terroristic violence in a relationship terrorism, or a man-caused disaster? This is a good place to consider the acronym KISS: *"keep it simple, stupid!"* Semantics get in the way by deflecting attention from the real issues. Arguing over words makes it harder to help people understand the problem and take action to correct it.

What one person calls abuse is violence to another. Someone else knows terror, and only sees violence as part of that experience, not terror. It is impossible and irresponsible to compare the impact of abuse, violence, or terrorism on any individual to that of another. Humans respond differently to different circumstances, and at different times in their lives. The effects of violence on human beings should never be minimized, whether domestic or social. It is not up to an observer's perception to define the impact of any act of violence on a human being. Only victims can do that.

OUT OF THE DIRT

Collette's family illness impacted hundreds of people over many generations. The practice of ghoulish rituals, inflicted unimaginable misery and sorrow on hundreds of innocent men, women and children for over a century. When the gruesome story of what took place in the small mountain town was finally exposed, shock and horror reverberated across the state. It was hushed up almost as quickly as it hit the news. An attempt was made to quell public anxiety and anger in the wake of arrests, and the macabre discoveries made in the town. Officials enforced a high level of secrecy around the case. In time, it simply went cold. Not only was there widespread disbelief of the evidence, there was *fear*. Fear that it was true.

We live in a very dangerous world. In a "live and let live culture", no one wants to throw stones. I won't rain on your parade if you don't rain on mine. Whistleblowers have a bad reputation. Snitches often suffer consequences detrimental to their health, if not life, for divulging information against others. That reality enables corruption and crime to flourish, and our culture to decline. Remaining loyal to honor and integrity is a hard road to tread. When called upon, however, most of us find the true grit that flows in our veins and turns us into faithful warriors. Sadly, for Collette there were no warriors of honor. It took her decades to face the demons that haunted her. She never stopped fearing for her life for telling her story.

That which is inherently good in human beings, our humanity, longs to connect with others. What is *not* good seeks relief from the pressure of its miserableness. Behind the masks cruel people wear, monstrosities lurk. Evil doesn't flinch, it waits patiently in the wings for its chance in the limelight. Undiscovered, the savage find their targets and destroy them. Recognizing and exposing evil is an obligation we must share.

A few years ago a friend confided information to me about a highly publicized murder. My friend was a wreck and needed to talk, but refused to go to the police. Lily (my name for her) was terrified because of what she knew. She desperately feared for her safety, and for her children. The man's death was a professional hit, and it was a nasty event. A bomb hidden in a gym bag on the front seat was remotely detonated shortly after he got into his car.

Debris from the explosion covered the parking lot of the posh resort he'd just left. It was also found a half mile away. He had been celebrating his birthday with friends. No one else was injured, but the blast could be heard for miles. The crime scene was macabre and offered little evidence for police and the FBI. Although a sordid collection of business associates and underworld figures were suspect, the case remained unsolved for years. The community was shaken by the awfulness of the crime and the lack of closure.

The situation was complicated for me. We all lived in the same city. While he was alive, my mother gave him music lessons, my son went to school with his daughter, and we boarded horses at the same barn. Every town is a small town at certain levels of society. Lily knew who was behind the assassination, and why. She'd heard it from-the-horse's-mouth, so to say, and believed she could be next on the list. The couple had an expensive lifestyle and a history of domestic abuse. Prior to their divorce, the marriage went on the rocks financially, but the wife owned a large insurance policy on her husband.

Years later, the hired killer was found, tried and sentenced to life in prison for the murder. He had been the ex-wife's lover, and the plot thickened as evidence tying her to the crime poured in. She disappeared with a couple million dollars of insurance money after paying him off. But despite extensive plastic surgery, her face was recognized in Europe from an Interpol poster. Shortly thereafter, the woman was extradited back to stand trial for the murder. What began as an abusive, chaotic, family in crisis, became an act of horrific societal violence. A lover turned hit man and a father was murdered and a family destroyed. The community looked on in horror.

Devastated friends, guests, employees, and law enforcement stood in the parking lot as the sirens rolled to a halt. Tiny pieces of an assassination lay before their disbelieving eyes. But Lily hid from it all. Her hair was falling out and she had debilitating panic attacks. My friend's own life was one of perpetual trauma and abuse. She knew the code of silence. Lily had been a battered spouse. Besides, she was exhausted. Her body couldn't tolerate the stress of getting involved. Hundreds, maybe thousands of people were affected by the crime. It was domestic violence that escalated to murder, but that detail wasn't mentioned. It's a detail that needs to be emphasized, not buried. But a sensational murder is far more curious than the fact that it was family violence.

When America was attacked by terrorists on September 11, 2001, we lost our innocence. The country was brutally awakened to a sober call for unity. From the ashes of terror, America rallied in communion of spirit to mend her broken heart. We rose to help the devastated and protect the nation from further assault. In the darkest moment of our modern history, we did not fail one another. That is what we are capable of when we turn into our task.

What you can do: Learn to see the connection between all forms of violence. Acknowledge the faces of darkness acting against us, whether in high places or the living rooms of our homes. Shine a light on the nature of violence and reject it. Refuse to tolerate violence and demand order and responsible behavior.

CHAPTER 7

A Tribal Nation

"He blew up my brains, but he didn't kill me. I just can't talk right anymore." The face of my new client was angrily contorted and flushed. He struggled for over a minute to speak those first few words to me. I remained silent, sensing his frustration. "I am a f-----g prisoner now!" he sputtered, stuck in the disconnect of severe cerebral impairment. Over the next long and arduous minutes, I was able to decipher what he was trying to say: "The creep shot a hole in my head, and now my brain is mush! My life is destroyed. I...don't even want to live anymore. I'm a vegetable. This is a joke. I hate all of you."

Dax was an athletic 24 year-old man attending college on the GI Bill. He'd been honorably discharged from the Army, but civilian life quickly became a problem for him. Seasoned by four years of soldiering, he found it difficult to relate to the other students. Most were still in their teens and being supported by parents. They didn't have to work. In his opinion, they were "spoiled, immature brats who just wanted to party." Dax found it especially hard to get along with coeds who expected him to spend a lot of money on dates. During the first semester he continued to binge drink on weekends like he did in the military. He also began using other drugs. Soon school, studying, and holding down a job began to conflict with his social life. Anger and resentment intensified as he struggled to keep it together.

There was continuous arguing with a new live-in girlfriend, Diana. Before long his agitation showed up at work. Finally, the daily problems with customers and co-workers created such a hostile environment that Dax was fired. He knew how to work, and found another job, but he was mad. He felt used by his girlfriend and unappreciated by employers. But he had his mind and was going to college. "Before this," he began, "the only thing I had going for me was my intelligence: I got straight A's... without studying. "Now that's gone. I have nothing. I wish he'd killed me," he blurted out, bitterness defining the moment.

An ugly incident with his girlfriend had erupted on the night of the shooting. The couple screamed the usual threats and obscenities at each other neighbors were used to hearing. As the two argued, Diana broke dishes and furniture, and Dax heaved beer bottles at the wall. In the rampage, she began hitting Dax with a boot for refusing to give her money for drugs. He heard sirens, but raced out of the apartment before the police arrived. Dax was evicted, and charged with criminal damage as well as domestic violence. Diana was charged as well, but left town.

It would be months before his arraignment on those charges could take place. He was in the hospital fighting for his life. Traumatic head injury, mental and physical impairment, and a future of rehabilitation rendered Dax incapable of fully understanding the situation he was in. When he finally appeared before the judge, Dax accepted responsibility for the argument and damaged property on advice of court-appointed legal counsel. Under the circumstances, prosecution offered diversion counseling in lieu of jail time. Dax agreed to the charges and left court facing the grim reality of his life. He paid a huge price for the choices he'd made.

As a result of the severe injury to his brain, thinking, speaking and writing were almost impossible for Dax. He would be in rehabilitation for years. Because he would not be able to fully participate in the interactive activities of a large class, a group diversion program was not an option for Dax. It was going to take a long-term, one-on-one counseling intervention to bring his mental and emotional abilities into focus. Violence was deeply imbedded in his brain. He was disabled, traumatized, and emotionally off the rails. Dax needed a second miracle. That he survived such a devastating injury was his first. It was my job to guide him toward the next.

The young man had serious problems long before he was shot. He found himself involved in conflict where ever he went. Throughout his childhood, a violent alcoholic father used beatings and relentless criticism to exact respect and obedience. "But I was smart.....by the time I was 12, I had figured out how to beat him at his game," Dax smirked, evidently enjoying what he was thinking. "I always had an extra bottle of booze hidden in my closet. All I had to do was shove it in his face when he went-off on me in one of his rages. He wanted hooch more than he wanted my ass. Worked every time. Trouble is," he paused, slouching down to lay his head back on the sofa. A torrent of tears streamed down his face.

"What trouble, Dax? Please go on," I encouraged.

"I hated him - hated everything about him....Was never going to be like him. Ever. I had a track scholarship waiting for me." My client raised his head and looked at me in utter sadness. "The problem was," he exhaled, blowing a long breath through tightly pursed lips. "It got to the point where there needed to be two bottles hidden in my room: one for him, and - *one for me!*" I blew it off. Blew off everything. Had to get away from him. My whole family was screwed up because of him. I just wanted out. So I enlisted. I was going to be a better soldier than he had been."

After the argument with Diana, Dax wound up down the street at a large fraternity party. Just minutes after walking into the crowd, he got into a brief, unprovoked altercation with a stranger. Suddenly, a lifetime of accumulated rage and violence was unleashed against an armed and homicidal drunk. Neither of them belonged to the fraternity or even knew anyone there. They were merely crashers, stumbling uninvited into the outdoor bash. A gun was drawn, and the close-range discharge of a .38 caliber bullet sped into Dax's forehead. It lodged deep in his brain. Residual fragments would impair his ability to think and speak for the rest of his life. The prognosis was dire. Our work together was challenging. It would last for five years.

The message of Dax's story is one of courage, character and the ability to heal. The man had every reason and opportunity to stay stuck in an enraged and bitter state. But he opted to be a victor instead of a victim. Quitting was not an option. Despite an abusive childhood, a history of violence, and permanent brain damage, he chose to rise above the pain. The anger caused by injury to his brain was at times insurmountable. Profound grief was sometimes inconsolable. When he lost himself along the way, Dax required temporary hospitalization and stronger medications to stabilize his behaviors and recharge his health. Relationships and menial jobs were impossible to maintain, as was abstinence from drugs and alcohol. He deeply resented authority, and local police knew him all too well. There were periodic scrapes with the law, and his odd behaviors often frightened people. But he stayed out of jail and stayed the course, guided by an inner force that wouldn't quit.

Over the years his family changed. They found their way back to each other and were able to begin the process of healing. It required years of family therapy, Alcoholics Anonymous, and lots of 'time out' to rest. With love and forgiveness, the tribe was strengthened and became the support the prodigal son needed on his difficult journey. Dax overcame his experience with the serpent because he refused to accept it in his life anymore. He spent time in treatment facilities and on probation. And there were always episodes of rage. Relationships came and went, and he moved from place to place. But he kept coming back.

Dax lived a chaotic, unstable life, struggling to think, speak, and stay out of trouble. He spent decades and most of his money fighting the demons that tormented him. Despite the odds, through hard work and relentless determination, Dax was graduated from college.

Remarkably, his grades were above average: in a rigorous four-year Bachelor of Science program. He landed a good job in his field, and continues to recover. Dax illustrates the undeniable courage of a hero." I never knew how I was going to get there," he once told me. "I just knew I would." His new life is a blessing; it is the second miracle.

HEROES OF DIFFERENT STRIPES

Old World explorers crisscrossed the earth on the tabs of wealthy crowns and rich patrons. They ignited the expansion of humanity and filled their coffers with plunder beyond comprehension. Legendary adventurers like Leif Erikson, Captain Cook, Christopher Columbus, Hernan' Cortez, Attila the Hun, Genghis Khan and millions of other unknown progenitors of our species partook of that bounty. Swashbucklers and pirates pillaged their way into history and are the fathers of modern civilization. They were nomadic tribesmen, and the seeds of their clans were planted around the world.

Through modern genetics, their migrations, and the races they created, are mapped beneath the celestial bodies that guided them. Like stars bursting into existence, new nations were birthed into creation. So too, the quest for power, control and sovereignty that would destroy them. Men departed their homelands for the perils of the unknown in a heightened mix of excitement and trepidation. They encountered war and devastation, natural disaster, and beauty. But pathfinders braved vast wildernesses and opened the way for others. They are the warriors and heroes of their time.

In the *Odyssey*, written by the Greek poet Homer over 2700 years ago, legends tell of adventures and wars between mythical creatures and mortal man. They remind us of our own struggles today.[1] Our true, basic selves haven't changed, only the stories have. We are like mythological heroes sailing across a world believed to be flat toward a horizon at the edge of the earth. Each of us face difficult rites of passage as we move along the continuum of life. It's important to find the inner heroes in ourselves. They are our personal bodyguards, the security protecting us from shipwreck on the turbulent seas of our lives.

Author Joseph Campbell described this rite in his monomyth called the *hero's journey*. In his classic book on comparative mythology, *The Hero with a Thousand Faces*, Campbell tells of brave men daring to venture from the comfort and safety of the *known* on a journey to the unknown.[2] Every storm endured and monster defeated, whether of natural or human origin, was a sacred badge of courage. It must have been exciting business. With every triumph, the bar of manhood by which all others would be measured was raised up a notch. Through endless struggle, men were brought face to face with a new way of seeing themselves and the world they lived in. But when heroes returned home, they discovered that home as they once knew it had also changed. It is the story of life from which the adage 'you can never go home' evolved.

But home is where the heart is. Coming home triggered the mechanism by which returning to their previous lives would be possible: *adaptation.* Those who couldn't, or wouldn't adapt to the changes at home failed to re-establish membership in the tribes that sustained them. Warriors who didn't fit in were a threat to the structural integrity of the clan, and were quickly ostracized. Only those able to adjust to their new lives or overthrow ruling chieftains were re-assimilated. Clan warfare and relationship violence was inevitable.

The hero's journey brought supernatural wonders never before experienced, and challenges never before attempted. Exhaustive tests of bravery forever changed the lives of ordinary men. In mythology, acts of heroism signified transcendence from ordinary to *extraordinary*. But great tales of courage among men could never have been written were it not for *women.* Childbearing women, the fecund cradles of civilization around the world, made such feats possible. They represent the other side of history: the *heroine's journey.* Together, heroes and heroines formed the union called family and the tree of life. Courageous women bore the offspring that defined the lineage of mankind and shaped the history of the world. In modern day culture, there is disagreement over the concept and definition of the heroine's journey. In reality, every man and every woman makes 'the journey'. It is uniquely personal and one of a kind. Like red hair: from carrot colored to burgundy, it's an amazing mystery.

House of Versace is a movie about the life and murder of famous couture designer, Gianni Versace.[3] Gianni's surviving sister and business partner, Donatella, had a vision for the revival of the devastated family's business after his death: "*Keep the identity, keep the DNA, but 'update'.*" It's a brilliant innovation that encompasses the power of love, family, and adaptation in the presence of adversity. The aftershock of murder in a family is immobilizing. There is no way to comprehend the degree of violence required to take a life. What remains is grief and anger.

Re-building life without the beloved family member is a crippling experience. Reserves of energy are depleted and difficult to refill. *Empowerment* became the mantra that would ring-in recovery for *Versace,* and the future of the brand's fashion collections. By embracing personal empowerment in the face of utter despair, Donatella brought new life to her designs and a sense of renewal to the millions of patrons who bought them.

Without resilience and the resolve to bounce back from the challenges life throws at us, we are doomed to the status quo. But having the ability to adapt doesn't mean we are *adept* at it. Proficiency at something requires practice and time. Veterans returning from the Viet Nam War during the 1960's and 1970's found American soil hostile territory. Young men and women put their lives on the line for country. When they returned home, soldiers were met with hatred and rejection. They were an army of mostly draftees, not volunteer enlistees, who honorably did their jobs.

Wounded, damaged, drug-addicted and fatigued, thousands of discharged soldiers crashed-landed back into a country that was no longer home, and a people who wanted to forget they existed. These warriors were not welcomed home; they were not called 'heroes'. The country was splintered by the political, social, and fiscal chaos that became known as the Viet Nam Era. An angry country and humiliated government recoiled in the aftermath of the tragic conflict. And a sub-culture of sex, drugs and rock and roll immersed itself in the excesses of self-indulgence. An entire generation of people continue to suffer the consequences and collateral damage of that apocalyptic war and period in our history. America was neither adept, nor did she ever fully adapt to the changes and sacrifices she made. It is an era warped with national shame because we failed as a nation to pull together, and to take care of our own.

Nothing stays the same; life is a process of transition. We are all aware of this fact, but change is uncomfortable and often resisted, rather than accepted. From daily 'little deaths' of what we are used to, to new beginnings, survivability is strengthened by the ability to adapt. Our survival as a great nation of tribes and individuals depends on our willingness as a whole to embrace this notion. Adaptability was the groundwork that animated the nations, tribes, and cultures from which we originate. The versatility of our ancestors runs thick in our veins today. The legacy of the hero's journey is the innate capacity of humans to collaborate with life and one another to achieve a positive outcome. We just have to decide to do it.

RITES OF PASSAGE

Organizations of all kinds establish rules and traditions, and to maintain a sense of cohesiveness. If membership is valuable, people will pledge loyalty, even their lives, to belong to them. In many cultures, disloyalty is punished in an effort to retain control. Whether in a country, homeowners' association, family, or club, some hold power, and others must obey. This is tribal justice, and at one level or another, it affects every man, woman, and child on the planet.

Athletic teams are tribal entities. Players earn positions and power according to their value in the hierarchy of the team. Team colors and player's numbers are worn with pride, and defended by the elite few selected to wear them. Victory and defeat define sport, just as sportsmanship defines an athlete. Loyalty isn't a matter of life or death, but fame, fortune and love of the game might be. New England Patriot tight end, Aaron Hernandez, embedded a plethora of tattoos in his flesh. But they proclaim allegiance to a darker level of tribalism, one far removed from the football club he represented.

Heavily tattooed skin is usually associated with gangs, drugs, and violence, according to law enforcement and hospital emergency rooms. Gang tattoos are the mark of fidelity and permanence. They broadcast membership in a club from which there is *no exit*. The game played by gangs is a pathological roulette of life and death. Hernandez denied gang membership. But photos of his cuffed hands at arraignment for the murder of his friend say something else. The word *BLOOD* was inscribed in red on the outer top of his right hand. Later, in a CBS interview, *it was gone*.[4] Showing up in a court of law wearing massive tattoos and a visible gang ID is not what one would expect of a non-member. It's also not what a *non-banger* would want to advertise to a judge if it wasn't true.

Whatever meaning the athlete's body art actually represents is unknown. But he is associated with a death. Police reports and inquiries on Hernandez show a history of violence. There is assault, domestic violence, and alleged involvement with other unsolved murders. The 23 year old has uncommon familiarity with guns, fights, and crime. Over time, more will be revealed. But the relationship between a history of violence and a first-degree murder charge is clear. An execution-style bullet (or three) to someone's head is the undeniable act if a sociopath. When violence is a lifestyle, it is not limited to family, gangs, and the neighborhoods controlled by it. It comes out in school, sports, and society, and ends up in prison.

Tats (tattoos) say something different in the primal culture of prison than they do in the hood or locker room. Gang culture is far more vicious in the Big House than on the street. Bad boys from other tribes are just waiting to get-it-on with new 'kids on the block', especially a famous one. The Rule of Law on the outside is the Rule of the Lawless on the inside. There is no exit from this culture either.

Prison exposes the tribal system at its worst. Adoring soldiers shield their heroes like pit bulls guarding a bone. But every step is measured against the weight and power of enemies. And *inmates* have all the time, and some of the most violent people in the world, at their disposal. Retaining power *is* the power, and isn't easily taken.

In this tale, a football star is a different kind of hero. One day he sat atop a star-studded pedestal of pigskin and gold. With the click of his cleats, he fell from Oz and returned to the violence of his childhood. It is a version of the hero's journey, but not one of a hero. Violence will always be a fact of life. Antiheroes can teach us how it works and what it looks like, if we are willing to see. Violent behavior is always based on power and control, whether in prison or in relationships. Murder is a teacheable moment for society. It is ultimate control.

THE WILD WEST RIDES AGAIN

Clear, simple rules that everyone understands make life flow more smoothly around the fire pit. An operating system, so to say. Indigenous tribes in America had those systems in place long before Europeans arrived. For thousands of years they managed land, crops, wildlife, families and life with intelligence and skill. Each nation had a system of survival. Tribes respected the wisdom of their ancestors, and the powers of nature. When those conditions ceased to be, so did the spirit at the center of their universe.

As a new nation, America was a free-for-all without restraint or limitation. Colonization, exploration and appropriation of land by immigrants exploded across the New Frontier. Settlers found their land, staked a claim, set up a lean-to and roughed out a new life. Today, still in diapers, relatively speaking, America is teetering once again on a new frontier. It is the Wild West of the New Millennium. We don't agree on very much of anything as a country. Disparate ideas divide us as we struggle to understand what has happened to us in the last few years.

When the 'not guilty' verdict was handed down in the trial of George Zimmerman, angry protesters across the country took to the streets. Throngs of people locked step in sometimes violent chants toward the man they called a child murderer. Outcry echoed in the late night and early morning hours outside the courthouse. Dissenters descended into the bright lights and microphones of the sympathetic media to express outrage. Accusations of racism surfaced. Protesters hurled epithets and charges of bias at the Criminal Justice System, the jury, and America in general. Before the evidence and case was even heard, they wanted a conviction.

For a year prior to the trial, angry protesters were systematically organized on the internet. Activists fired people up with the promise of justice for the dead teenager. In the heat of the pre-trial chaos, some heavily funded political groups and government officials voiced biased judgments. A cable news station admitted lying and corrupting evidence in the case before releasing it to the public. It was an energy reminiscent of the racial tensions and protests of the 1960's. The case became a vehicle of hostility and violence for an angry people seeking vengeance instead of due process.

Before the trial began, bounties were posted on the internet offering $10,000 rewards, "dead or alive," for the shooter, Threats of death, retaliation and violence were levied against Zimmerman, his family, and his legal team. In the year of mourning after the shooting, the parents of the dead teenager traveled extensively, both nationally and internationally. Enormous sums of money and sympathy were collected in the wake of the tragic loss of their son. They registered trademarks in the young man's name. *Trayvon* became a brand for proprietary use in the production and sales of clothing and other items in his memory.[5] The family allegedly hired dozens of attorneys and advocates to provide counsel, marketing and financial services throughout the trial. A system was put in place. A clan was empowered, profit hustlers got rich, emotions flared, and the potential for violence grew.

Everyone grieves differently. But an organized effort to legitimize *hate* is not a grieving process. It is societal violence. The case was pre-judged on the street, in the media, and on the internet before it even reached the court. In an egregious show of mobocracy, crowds of children and adults chanted and rapped incessantly, declaring the defendant guilty and convicted. Protestors showed shameful disregard for the concept of 'innocent until proven guilty', the credo at the heart of American Justice. Grieving family members on both sides of the courtroom were harassed by opportunists. For days following the verdict, rioters slashed and burned their way across the country in retaliation. People who respect one another do not act this way. Such protests should not be confused with Freedom of Speech or any other freedom. It is the behavior of a culture out of control.

Trayvon had a history of violence. Problems at school, fights, drugs, and possible gang associations depict a troubled teen. Angry videos and pictures of Trayvon posted on the internet defy innocence and youth.[6] Violence went viral in this case, from home, to society, to the worldwide web. Zimmerman also had a history of domestic violence. Death concluded one of those histories, and exposed the other to the world. But the point is made: Profiles of these individuals reveal extensive involvement with violence as a way of life. Violence isn't cute, it isn't 'kids being kids,' it isn't justified, it isn't racial, it is social deterioration.

Profiling is maligned and viewed incorrectly by many as an ugly, unacceptable activity. Identifying people by traits and specific characteristics in a nervous culture terrified of being politically incorrect, racist or bigoted, has created a culture of fear. It is fear that prevents *saying something when you see something*. Something said, and corrective actions taken, may have prevented this tragedy.

In *Bullies: How the Left's Culture of Fear and Intimidation Silences America,* author Ben Shapiro explains the reality of social repression.[7] The power and oppression of popular opinions sometimes goes too far, even when those opinions represent the beliefs of the minority of people in America. Bullies can be uncompromisingly aggressive and disturbing to ordinary people. Few people are willing to take the risk of disagreeing or standing up for their beliefs in the scary atmosphere of social abuse and bullying in America today.

As a fact of life, profiling is exactly what we do - every one of us, every time we make a judgment. There are hundreds of invisible filters in our minds that organize the information and experiences we have gathered in life from birth. We filter information through these conscious and unconscious sieves as we receive it. Our mental filters summarize the inflow of facts that constantly impact our decisions, perceptions, beliefs and lives. We judge, profile and discriminate our way through any given day every minute we are awake.

Familiar words like 'brand, tattoo, colors, (as in gang affiliation), personnel file, Facebook, resume, employment or loan application, gender, marital status and prefix and surname' are all examples of profiling. They are identifiers, used to describe. A driver's license, passport, birth certificate and actor's or modeling portfolio all provide information with which to identify someone by utilizing profiling. As a culture feverishly focused on correctness, we ignore the obvious necessity and usefulness of profiling.

Profiling is an accurate means of classification that has been defamed. Hyper-sensitive individuals and groups want to control what others say and do. It's a power grab and an ill-informed attempt to prevent hurt feelings. In reality, someone is going to be 'offended' by someone in some way, no matter what. Most people understand this rationale. Reason and common sense deliver us from the obsessive idea that we can prevent people from feeling hurt or offended. We are all subject to someone's judgment or profiling. It's not only dishonest, it is ragingly codependent to pretend we aren't.

Making healthy observations and judgments about what is going on around us is common sense. Anyone who has taken a self-defense class is taught to profile. What is a self-defense class for? *To learn how to avoid being attacked, and how to defend yourself if you are.* Paying attention to faces, eyes, body language, expression, voice, movement and other clues alerts us to potential threat. Gathering information helps defend against harm. Without the ability to profile and make sound judgments, people perish.

Ours is a nation of many tribes. Per capita, the United States opens her doors to more immigrants than any other country in the world. America used to be a melting pot. We came here to be *Americans together,* not separate bands and tribes. Neighbors learned to coexist and respect differences. Such diversity and multi-culturalism makes us great, but it has also made us vulnerable. Values and ethics continue to decline as a secular culture replaces traditional values and principles. People are reticent to speak up for their rights and beliefs. Demanding recognition and observance of separate rules, beliefs, and cultures is crazy-making. One nation, not ten thousand, stabilizes a country.

MARKING TERRITORY

The girls and woman held captive by Ariel Castro in a quiet Ohio neighborhood were victims of the worst kinds of domestic violence and 'family abuse'. It took place for years, right under the noses of nearby neighbors and extended family members. Strange activities behind the high fence that encircled the partially boarded up house of the alleged abuser failed to attract questions or concern by unsuspecting neighbors. Even family members who knew about his history of domestic violence were unaware of the evil that resided in the home. Nobody knew. Castro inflicted horrendous abuse on many people during his years as a free man. Yet he persisted, unchecked by any one.

When children or adults are abducted and held hostage against their will, they have been forced into a domestic relationship with their captor. As sinister and horrifying as that fact is, the crime has in fact established a relationship that is, by definition, 'domestic'. Once individuals live in residence with each other, they are in a de facto *domestic relationship,* regardless of how they got that way, voluntarily or involuntarily.

The actual place of domicile may be a gruesome imprisonment, but it is 'home' to a hostage for however long their abductor wishes or they survive. Once taken, kidnap victims lose all power and control over their lives. They are in the possession of a master. From that moment on, existence depends on the intentions of the keeper. Whatever survival instincts a captive may have are secondary. Critical, yes, but extinguishable in the hands of an abuser. If sexual assault occurs during the imprisonment of a kidnapping victim, the violation forms yet another connection between the abductor and the victim. They now have intimacy, not just co-habitation. Once this takes place, possession is consummated. *The reptile has marked his territory*. Rape finalizes the master-slave bond.

And last, but most importantly, a child conceived from the rape of a kidnap victim establishes a permanent link between the rapist and his victim. Throughout the history of humankind, the creation of a child has marked the flow of genes and traits that have led to evolution. With the addition of the child to the equation, the three have become members of the same clan. His forced paternity has created a new life, but the act is really a *devolution* of the will and body of his victim.

It is a bastardization of the word to view such an outcome as *family*. The precious bond between parent and child is established in violence, but it has made a family, nonetheless. The new relationship between them is by blood, not just by domicile or forced intimacy. And a pure and innocent life has been created and placed in the cradle of life. The child is carrying the combined nuclear DNA of its victimized mother, and its diabolical father. Sadly, there are now two victims, mother and child. In the sacrilege that brought them together they are forever linked to the gene pool of their shared assailant. They are a tribe.

NOBODY NOTICED

"I did it, Donna, I really did it! *I killed him* last night. *I slit his throat*!" Sandi's calm but high-pitched voice was clear and proud. I was speechless, and dropped into a chair. "He's dead. Connor is finally *dead*!!" Her name popped up on my caller ID, so I was sure it was my client, but this wasn't the Sandi I knew. The petite, chain-smoking, big rig driving grandmother wasn't capable of murder - was she? "He broke into the truck just like he did before, and this time I had my hunting knife in bed with me. It was so dark, he didn't see it in my hand. I just reached up and slashed it across his neck, Donna. It was real fast!" Sandi was excited now, and the image in my mind left me numb. Silence.

"Hello?" she said, hoping I was still there.

"I'm listening Sandi," my voice croaked.

"I mean, not really-I didn't *really* kill him, it was just a dream! *I did it in my dream*, Donna, not for reals! *Please believe me*... But it was horrible. It was so real... it terrified me. I finally stopped him, and it feels so strange...and it's weird... I had to call and tell you. It was only a dream. But I killed my abuser, and I don't have to go to prison for it! Hahahahaha!" Sandi was elated. She was swimming in a surreal state of un-reality. My heart stopped fluttering like a chicken's, and my lungs filled with air again. Grandma wasn't a murderer.

Sandi had a horrible marriage to a truck driver. She fell in love with the man and with trucking while traveling with him in his 18 wheeler. After they married, she got licensed and worked hard to get into her own rig. But Connor hated her independence, and was violently jealous. Their routes often crossed, and he would find out where she was and drive all night to track her down. One night, as she slept in the cab at a remote truck stop, Connor broke into the cab. Before she knew it, he was beating her viciously. Then he raped her. The rampage put Sandi in the hospital so severely injured it nearly took her life. Although she drove a big rig, she was tiny and delicate. There had been lots of grief and misery in her childhood and most of her adult life. A marriage, three kids, a divorce, and some grandchildren later - she met Connor.

The man was younger, handsome, and very big. He could charm the birds off a tree and then uproot the tree in one fell swoop. At least, he looked like he could. And he swept her off her feet with money, gifts, and constant attention. Unfortunately, Connor was a spoiled brat with multiple drug addictions and severe mental illness. His rap sheet was long and harsh. Woman after woman filed police reports of domestic violence against him. They ran for their life. The night he assaulted Sandi, nobody saw what happened. She was alone for hours in the darkness of a bloodied truck after he disappeared. By daybreak, she was barely able to move. Another driver walking by heard the tapping of her ring on the window of the sleeper.

The hospital called the police, and a report was filed. They put out a BOLO (be on the lookout) for him, and the hunt for her husband was on. Beside the fact that the man was very mentally ill, what made Connor especially dangerous was his job. He was never in the same state for more than a day or two. And because he was a good driver, he crossed the country unnoticed. Wherever he went, there were fights and beatings but he always got away before he was caught. But beating Sandi was a serious felony. In a few months, they had him. Two years later he was released from prison and wanted Sandi back. She was weak, and he was *so, so sorry*, and it would never, ever happen again, he told her. She was too scared to refuse him. They nestled into her cab and set off on the next delivery far across the country. And it happened again.

"I can't take it anymore, Donna." She cried. It was several years earlier, and the first time we talked. "He's calling and texting and threatening to kill me if I don't come back! I don't know what to do!"

Sandi wanted a divorce, but Connor was after her and crazed-out on drugs. Her life was in extreme danger. The courts were not going to put him away this time. He was too difficult to jail; too many mental problems, advocates pleading mercy, and too much money on his side to put him behind bars. The family was well-to-do, and bailed him out of trouble for decades. "Everyone has a price," his father told me. "I love the kid." In truth, dad was also afraid of Connor. When he didn't get his way, the tyrant destroyed furniture and cars, and pushed his old man around. It always worked. Sisters and brothers kissed up to him, providing money or drugs when he demanded them. The clan was in crises when Connor was in town. Treatment facilities, hospitals, overnight jail stays, probations and medication failed to straighten him out. But there was no stopping him. He was a walking bomb always ready to explode.

Sandi's dream had been an imaginary act of extreme violence. But we both understood it completed the painful process of healing. We had worked together on many levels to process through the destructive PTSD she suffered. One of the most significant skills she developed was dream journaling. Identifying the clearest parts of her dreams, the feelings she experienced with them, and understanding *why*, empowered her. Each new dream brought greater clarity and progress. This one was the final step in releasing the fear that held her hostage.

Sandi is a heroine. She gave up living in fear to reclaim her life. Many traumas had crushed her heart and damaged her body. But she fought her way back and stopped bending to violence. She found social and legal resources to help, stayed busy on the job, and finally got her divorce. It took guts and time, but she persisted, and Connor left her alone. Different versions of Sandi's story are repeated over and over as domestic violence continues to escalate. With no boundaries or limitations to stop them, abusers like Connor float through society with ease.

More women are being battered, and more males are becoming batterers. Domestic violence is a national crisis. Boys grow up in homes where violence against women is not only tolerated, but expected and endorsed. Girls learn that male abuse of females is acceptable. In homes where girls witness mothers and sisters being victimized, as well as themselves, abuse becomes normal. The potential for abused girts to grow up and partner with abusive men is very great. Abused women and abusive men produce angry, abusive little boys, and more abusable little girls. And the violence goes on without end.

Pathologies and psychiatric disorders often arise in children, especially males, raised in violent or abusive households. They seem to potentiate the risk factors seen in individuals who go on to commit social violence and terrorism, as well as domestic abuse. We can't predict or prevent any of these forms of terrorism. But we have the ability to break down the traits, characteristics and overt (open), or covert (secretive) clues given out by potential offenders. *Profiling* specifically for those traits and clues may help us to mitigate the risk they pose. Dax showed the signs of risk by age 12, when he began drinking, but they went unnoticed at school, in sports, and in the military. He hid them well.

As J. Reid Malloy, Ph.D., writes, we can learn to trust our emotional reactions and anxiety, wariness, and fear around people who seem to be acting and talking in frightening ways. A certain amount of vigilance and attention with factual profiling may save a life, Malloy asserts. All we have to do is pay attention and then let law enforcement do their work.[8] It is that whole issue of paying attention that we are being shunned from doing by deciding that doing so somehow violates others. So when a man sitting on a crowded San Francisco passenger train pulled out a gun and started waving it around, not once, but many times, nobody noticed.[9] Even when he used the barrel of the loaded handgun to scratch his nose, no one saw him do it! Or, at least, no one did anything about it.

Oblivious and completely absorbed in their laptops, phones, readers and stuff, passengers were unconscious to the blatant danger just inches away. According to the train's videos, at least a dozen or more people in the car remained so engrossed in their devices they failed to even look up during the trip. Any one of them would have seen the gun-wielding man who was becoming increasingly agitated as the train sped to its destination.

When the train stopped, the gunman followed a 20 year old college student as he de-boarded. Coming up behind him, he pulled out his gun and shot him in the back. As Dr. Malloy cautions, the murder might not have happened if so many people had not been so utterly disconnected from their surroundings and each other as they sat crowded together on the train. Investigation of the shooter revealed a house filled with knives and weapons of all kinds. It was apparently a random kill, but a planned one. And nobody noticed - until it was done.

Hidden as domestic, social, and terrorist violence, the serpent awaits his opportunity, and when we're not paying attention, he strikes. The newest violence to hit our streets is the game called *Knock Out,* a.k.a., *Knock Out King.* According to The Washington Times and other news sources reporting on its increasing popularity among teens, the goal of the game is to select a random victim passerby and knock him out with a single punch. That punch is called "the one bitter quitter". Players refer to the game as "fun," a "joke!" Groups of teen 'hitters' have been roving the streets of New York City, New Jersey, and Washington, D.C. in broad daylight to find people to take out. Anyone, anywhere is vulnerable to this violent blitzkrieg assault that comes out of nowhere.

YouTube videos show victims, including males, females, elderly people and mothers with children, struck and dropped in these crimes. Some have died. That such games even exist is unconscionable. That these assaults are videoed, uploaded to the internet, and spread virally around the world should strike terror in our hearts. The question of who is responsible for domestic and social violence in America is uncomfortable and emotionally charged. But it is a question that must be answered. It isn't enough to feel disgusted, offended, shocked, or afraid; *violence requires corrective action.*

Domestic violence cannot be confined. It slips out of its nest through doors and windows and infects the world around us. It shows itself on our faces, in our moods and in the words we speak. It is twisted and deformed, and coils in our guts ready to strike. Violence renders us either prey, predator... or *both.* Without resistance to its power, it creeps into our lives and corrupts our families. We may witness its effects and feel it seething around us, but we fail to understand the damage it does.

What you can do: Find the hero inside. You have untapped courage and energy to pursue your dreams, and travel your journey. Be willing to say what you think and believe, and stand up for your rights. Look in your family and identify your tribe. Get involved and take action to correct areas of your life that need improvement.

CHAPTER 8

How Did We Get Here?

Not overnight. Ten years ago, teenage girls reported what they valued in their life was kindness and consideration. Today, according to a UCLA study, those values have been replaced by "fame, celebrity and financial success".[1] Like the lyrical expose' on materialism suggested in Madonna's popular 1984 song, Material Girl, living in a material world has changed who we are, and what we care about. It is a change in the very heart of America: *our values.* It's a good thing young women aren't putting value on kindness or consideration in their lives today. They are uncommon traits difficult to find.

Instead of kindness and consideration, there is an abundance of anger. Pop culture music reveals a side of America that condones the expression of vulgarity and violence, especially toward women. It is far from the sensual *torch songs* of the 1940's, and the soft, romantic love songs crooned in the 1950's that filled hearts with hopes and dreams. A paradigm shift has taken place in the American songbook. Like movies and television, our music is a snapshot of society at any given moment in time. Music speaks to us about our lives and relationships using language that defines who we are. The denigration of women in *Gangsta Rap* is a terrible warning of the way things are, and where we are going as a culture.

When super star Aretha Franklin sang the words *"R-E-S-P-E-C-T, find out what it means to me!"* in her 1967 hit by that title, there was no question what she meant. Released during the intense era of the feminist and civil rights movements, the song became an anthem for activists as they fought for change in the turmoil of a splintered, war-torn country. Women marched and lobbied for their rights, and segregation ended, but all the protests in the world could not, in the end, prevent the fallout that had darkened that decade: our socio-cultural breakdown. A new era of freedom was underway, and with it, a threatening monster was about to emerge from its cave.

The country turned on itself as it recoiled from the explosive impact of political dissent, and a drug-laced, counter-culture, hell-bent on freeing itself from traditional values took to the national podium. Although a small percentage of the population renounced the America of their parents, their voices became a loud, squeaky wheel. Four decades later we are living the consequences of that social revolution. Voracious free love, drugs and activism powered much of the 1960's. Civil crises, social unrest, racism, war and violence continue to dominate the American landscape today. Progressive movements intended to spread sunshine and rainbows across a disenfranchised land also had a darker side. Instead of pots of gold under the colorful rainbows, we found *cultural poverty*.

By attempting to unchain us all from the suffocating tentacles of the evil American empire it sought to transform, a liberated generation had unleashed a demon from its lair: the serpent in the house-domestic violence. While we were busy pursuing our lives, the clash of old and new values began to reframe our ideas about relationships and society. The complicated fretwork of change ushered in splintered families, latchkey children and social confusion. Men and women no longer had clearly defined roles, and children were no longer perceived as needing both a mommy *and* a daddy in their lives. In fact, children themselves were no longer necessary. Relationship violence was kept private behind the closed doors of earlier generations. In the light of the new dawn of male and female emancipation it suddenly went public.

As millions of female baby-boomers moved into the male-dominated workforce, gender conflict and shattering glass ceilings rendered many households less than harmonious. For liberated women trying to "have it all," and men trying to figure out what was happening, home sweet home was a battlefield. And for millions of children caught in the crossfire of domestic pandemonium, divorce, and the daily stress of single-parent households, the American family faded into history at warp speed.

Over the past few decades, the unwanted shackles of personal morality and accountability have been replaced by permissiveness. We have produced and re-produced a populace of supremely ego-centric hedonists for whom being free to be and do whatever they want is all that matters. Reckless seeds of narcissism sprouted the chaos of our culture today. They were planted in the fertile soil of social upheaval. That we find ourselves a country held hostage to the repetitive tragedies of relationship, societal, and terrorist violence should come as no surprise. We are reaping what we have sown.

In today's vernacular, long after Aretha asked for a little re-spect, the word *disrespect* is more common. It is so popular it morphed into "*dissed*". Most of us experience a "dis" or two on a regular basis without a problem. We simply shrug it off and consider the source rather than taking it too seriously. But for the more emotionally fragile, to be disrespected is to be dishonored - the most unforgiveable form of disrespect. Dishonoring is viewed by angry people as a personal offense. It has to be avenged to regain their damaged honor. Revenge is a highly destructive use of energy because it sets in motion the signature pathology of all forms of violence: the *cycle* of violence. Instead of settling a conflict, a vengeful act of pay-back inevitably leads to more violence.

We are in a perpetual state of social unrest because somebody is always feeling abused or disrespected and demanding special privilege.

It is an unsettling aspect of our culture that undermines our sense of national unity because it empowers a sub-culture of self-identified victims. Because Americans have been conditioned to cater to this special class of victims in order to avoid being labeled insensitive or bigoted, we don't know how we are supposed to think or act any more.

When the police photo of Rihanna, the beautiful girlfriend of rapper Chris Brown, went viral on the internet, it was not pretty. Her face was drawn, cut and bruised from the violent assault she claimed she had endured from her lover in a fit of rage. Like many famous people, Brown's charisma and massive popularity have shielded him from a major fall from grace. The disclosed abuse of his lady, and the many other alleged assaults and charges he got before going into re-hab didn't, touch him. An angry rapper's true claim to fame **is** his anger. Violence-driven tunes make tons of money because they are idolized by millions of vulnerable fans to whom criminal behavior is not only no big deal, it is a lifestyle they relate to.

Repetitive, angry lyrics are capable of desensitizing some individuals to violence in the same way violent video games, television and movies are. At the opposite extreme, violent music, games, television and movies are capable of *igniting* violence in disturbed people. In either case, the response to violence becomes unremarkable. Cultural desensitization produces mass antipathy, especially in young people. When the diva was asking for respect, Elvis gyrated to All Shook Up, and the Beatles sang about Michelle, violence was not the message being drilled into the skulls of their shrieking, tear-soaked, audiences. Today, violence is a pervasive message being pumped out across a plugged in society.

BUT IT'S THE GUNS, STUPID!

"My boy is a baby," the mother of the alleged teen shooter of the young Australian jogger, Christopher Lane, professed adamantly. "I know my son. He is a good kid."[2] There is no such thing as a good kid at home but a killer on the street. There are always red flags. But those closest to them don't, or won't, see them.

After playing violent video games for hours, three teens said they were *bored*, and decided to get in the car and find someone to kill "for the fun of it". Lounging around and smoking pot, with nothing to do, access to guns, a car, and no parents asking questions, the gangsta threesome took off. "Two drops in two hours," they latter bragged, talking about their plans for the afternoon thrill-seeking killing spree. The teens didn't mean two drops of blood, they meant two bodies. But they were caught before they made the second drop.

Aussie media reported on the tragedy angrily pronouncing "lax gun laws" as the cause of crime in America. Despite some of the strictest gun laws on the planet, Australia has a history of high per capita gun crimes that belie that claim. But it's easier and more sensational to assign America's crime problems to our constitutionally protected rights than to look deeper for the truth. Superficial explanations keep the fires of denial alive for people afraid or incapable of honesty. When tragedy strikes, it is human nature to see only the edges around it instead of the high definition reality in the center. America's problems stem from lax families, lax values, lax courts and lax enforcement of the Rule of Law, not our 2nd Amendment rights.

Within hours of the murder, the Herald Sun in Australia published photos of the three suspects. Not one of the U.S. media did. Political correctness and an unwillingness to see the issue of American black teen violence for what it is kept media quiet. Neither the President, the Attorney General, Civil Rights leaders, nor Hollywood activists usually irate and vocal about social justice and civil rights, acknowledged the case of the black teens. They choose to look the other way. The reason for the proliferation of America's violence is the demise of the family and fundamental cultural values.

Drug use and de-criminalization of marijuana have radically contributed to the loss of our social foundation. Colorado struggles with the mess they created. Personal possession, medical use, growers and retailers saturate the pristine air of the Rockies with Ganga. The state is overrun with potheads. High unemployment, crime and the classic malaise of the stoner have not produced the happy outcome voters had hoped for. Neighborhoods and law enforcement face dangerous turf wars, robberies and the influx of unsavory outsiders and cartels involved in the drug world. But the state collected a lot of new tax money, new residents, and visitors.

Enter the District of Columbia, our nation's capital, where the unemployment rate is 8.7%, and the teen unemployment rate is a whopping 50.1%. It is a district, not a state, with a population of just over 632,000, but the rate of use of marijuana in Washington is the third highest in the country-and growing. The arrest rate for blacks in D.C. is over 8 times that of whites-leading the nation in per capita arrests - with the U.S. Census Bureau reporting the population at 50% African-American. In response to vehement demands for justice from civil liberties groups, legislators and voters, the Department of Justice decriminalized the personal possession of small amounts of marijuana in the District.

Because the huge majority of arrestees and incarcerations for possession of marijuana in D.C. are black, the Attorney General has deemed the ratio unjustly biased and ordered the laws changed to correct the statistic and level the playing field. Local Councilmembers extolled the benefits of legalizing the drug because prohibitionist laws and arrests have been destroying African-American families. So, let's get this straight: *getting high and dumbed down, de-motivated, unemployed, memory-challenged, paranoid, addicted and living a lifestyle persistently under the influence of a carcinogenic hallucinogen are not the reasons for high arrests and broken families: it is discrimination and social injustice that is to blame!*

Grant Smith, policy manager with the Drug Policy Alliance office of National Affairs, a loud voice for decriminalization of marijuana, also hopes that D.C. will in the future look to decriminalize all drug possession as well. Smith believes that "ultimately, drug use is most effectively addressed as a health issue instead of as a criminal justice issue"[3]. In 2012 violent crime in D.C. surged, spiking sharply with a 40% increase. According to the FBI, the murder rate in the capital ranks 8th among the country's cities with populations over 500,000.

Gun control advocates agree that the capital has some of the strictest gun laws in the country, yet robberies and murders using firearms are on the increase.

It doesn't take a genius to connect the dots. When our elected leaders fail to protect millions of Americans by enacting laws based on politics and special interests instead of our national welfare, it is testimony to a violation of their fiduciary responsibility to us. Softness on crime is a national disaster that has insinuated itself into the courts of every state. There is relentless pressure by civil rights activists to minimize or eliminate mandatory sentencing for "non-violent" crimes like drug offenses. Their argument is that this is a category of offenders that are "non-violent and low-level" who require treatment, not incarceration.

After 28 years of working with drug offenders, I am at a loss to comprehend a mind that is capable of rationalizing that drug-involved crimes are *non-violent* and *victim-less*. Truth may be in the eyes of the beholder, but the blind do not want to see.

KROKODIL

It turns your skin as green, scaly and tough as the animal it is named after, the *crocodile*. That's because it's a flesh-eating monster that consumes its host from the inside out, rotting bone, organs and tissue at the sight of injection with irreversible gangrene.

Krokodil is a low quality black-market street drug that first got attention in 2010 when vendors began making it in Russia. It is a home-made drug synthesized from codeine, using iodine and red phosphorous, in a process similar to making methamphetamine. Ingredients like oil, paint thinner, alcohol, gasoline and whatever other corrosive toxic materials are available are also thrown into the mix. The product is a version of *desomorphine*, an opioid derivative of morphine first patented in the United States in 1932, and used as a fast-acting sedative and analgesic.

Krokodil is easily made and ready to use in 30 minutes. The drug's effect is similar to heroin, but differs in a horrifying way. Three out of a hundred heroin addicts can be cured. But if the first slam of *krokodil* into a vein doesn't cause instant death, the life-expectancy of a heavy *k*-addict is just 2-5 years. *Krokodil kills all of its users.* Disfigured addicts have been turning up in emergency rooms across America in increasing numbers. In the most severe cases, treatment is limited: amputation of gangrenous flesh and limbs where possible, pain management, or, end-of-life care.

It is cheap, available, insanely addictive, and it is already in or coming soon to your neighborhood. In a culture going light on drug use, crime and punishment, deadly substances like Krokodil are likely to ease quickly into the already vast inventory of the American drug culture. The solution is not more legalization or political and legal advocacy.

The wildly popular television series, *Breaking Bad,* dramatized the story of Walter White, a chemistry teacher gone bad. White manufactured *blue meth*, a meticulously produced drug he created in his state-of-the-art lab. Crystal meth (methamphetamine) is a major cause of permanent disability, mental illness and death among its users, many of whom are teenagers. 'Tweakers', addicts easily recognized by their grossly conspicuous mental, motor and physical impairment, are everywhere. The massively debilitating effects of bathtub-meth have swept through virtually every state, causing devastating results for families, communities, law enforcement and the health care industry, yet it prevails.

"Chemistry is the study of transformation!" Walter White arrogantly declared while stashing millions of dollars from his deadly blue creation. Sadly, the transformations the chemistry of drug and alcohol abuse are causing in our country today are *not the droids we are looking for*, to quote the line from Star Wars. Contrary to the ill-informed and mistaken proponents of victim-less crime, there is no such thing when it involves illegal drugs and drug use. Abuse of prescription drugs now kills more people in the U.S. than any other substances. Addiction to narcotics and controlled pharmaceuticals of all kinds is rampant at all socio-economic levels, and it is a *big* industry not going away anytime soon.

With the aggressive pursuit of legalization and de-criminalization of marijuana and other substances by activists, voters and local and federal governments. America is witnessing virtual mass spiritual suicide as more children, teenagers and adults step into the world of drugs. Addiction is a disease of the spirit, and we are becoming a spiritually bereft nation of addicts. Drugs and alcohol are a crutch often used by angry people. Violence is exaggerated with the use of mood altering substances. So is suicide and homicide. Nothing good will come of more drugs and more drug users in a society already broken down.

SCREAMING FOR ATTENTION

Children are most vulnerable to chaotic environments. There has been a 72 percent increase in the number of homeless children in the United States over the past few years, with 1.2 million living in shelters, motels and with relatives instead of in their own homes. It is estimated that 15 percent of all young people ages fifteen to twenty-four are neither in school nor working. Kids have smart phones, social media and video games, but little supervision. High school drop-out rates and low test scores tell the story of failed parenting, education and the absence of motivation. Flash mobs, gangs, drugs and violence are the social play pens of our abandoned youth.

Effective communication skills are essential to any successful relationship, and for many of us, especially younger generations, our bond with social media forms the basis of not only *how* we communicate, but *what*. USA News reported on a study that identified anger as *the most powerful emotion on the internet today.*[3] Dispositions, like anger and laughter, are easily spread from individual to individual. Because millions of people have significantly strong relationships to social media, the expression of anger is capable of spreading over the entire planet like a contagious disease.

Studies have compared the viral spread of online feelings to the phenomena of *"irresistible sicknesses"*. In very much the same way that intensely itchy skin makes scratching it irresistible, watching acts of violence induces irresistible anger in the viewer. In each case, we have the makings of physical or mental sickness.

A Chinese study found that the internet has the capacity to amplify negative emotions. Participants studied spewed out angry epithets and feelings at their computer screens more often and more easily in the safety of the internet than in other face to face interactions. The hypothesis, "solipsistic interjection", infers that chatting on the internet is more similar to subconsciously talking to ourselves than with a live human being. In our 'virtual invisibility', we are anonymous and dissociated.[4] "The more expansive the field of influence, such as Facebook, Twitter, blogs, etc., the greater the enhancement of an expressed emotion".

Regular uninhibited expressions of anger set quickly in motion across the internet with just a few keystrokes could potentially activate worldwide stress-response to that emotion, according to researchers. The power of that effect was attributed to a video alleged to have ignited the violence in the Middle East that led to the brutal assassinations of Americans in Benghazi, Libya. Appropriated to serve a purpose that benefitted a political agenda of darker intentions, that story was later exposed as a monumental untruth. But the damage had already been done.

The powerful impact and danger posed by the dissemination of negative emotions via the Ethernet became horribly clear to a world naively caught in that unfortunate media spin. Fortunately, the same heavily-muscled field of influence across the internet holds true for the expression of *positive* emotions. Happiness, humor and love are medicine for our souls, and we instinctively know that. YouTube abounds with videos depicting stories of animals and people that delight our souls and offer light-hearted distraction whenever we wish. Humans like feeling good, and global media offer magnum doses of laughter and the opportunity to revel in the greatness of goodness and the beauty of nature.

Rant sites didn't even exist a few years ago. Now, when we are alone in front of a screen, we can privately issue our primal scream at the world by visiting a rant room and letting off steam. A deep, guttural shout of unbridled rage into the Ethernet will certainly clear out the sinuses, but it does much more to us than we think. In studies conducted by the University of Wisconsin, Green Bay, on why people express themselves on rant sites, researchers came up with interesting outcomes. Studies found that rant-sites provided not only a venue for venting, but also the creation of a *sense of shared experience.*[5]

Beyond the venting and sharing, however, their studies also found that people were more likely to feel *worse in the long term* for their rant experiences, not better. Anonymity of posters opened previously checked floodgates of vitriolic expression that would normally have been kept shut if their true identities had been revealed. This is classic cowardice. It is a serpent of another kind, an abuser, nonetheless. Rant sites may be the new 'empty chair' or 'bataka' anger therapy models of the 1990's, updated for the techno world. But in a Psychology Today article by Natalie Nahal, "Rant sites do us harm," the impact of the experience of visiting rage sites was not positive. It was a level of 'e-harm' that potentiated the venting of anger in other areas of life, and with real people.

Virtual explosions, bullying, harassment and abuse can easily become common behaviors in an angry individual. With no discipline or reserve in place to curb explosive emotions on the internet, little or no restraint is in place that would prevent the same outbursts in actual face-to-face encounters. At home and in public, whether on the phone, on the road or at the grocery store, it has become more common to experience people popping off with whatever comes into their minds. More adults and children are being involuntarily exposed to other people's personal business and dysfunction than a decade ago, as public rudeness continues to increase and multiply around our lives.

CONSCIOUS CONSCIENCE

One morning my 9 year-old son called me from the principal's office at his grade school. In a high and obviously excited voice, he blurted out a short question: "Mom, is it alright if I punch Anthony in the nose?" He was out of breath and in a hurry, continuing before I could respond. "He's teasing me and my friends and I hate him!" I didn't want to laugh at my son, but it was pretty funny that he would first call and ask me for permission to beat Anthony up. I was quite sure he hadn't told the office secretary why he needed to phone home, but could only imagine her face as she listened to his call.

My son had a conscience, but it was getting in the way of what he consciously really wanted to do: punch the other kid's lights out. Calling mom for permission to inflict pain on Anthony gave him an excuse to make his case for the use of violence to shut the kid up. Calling mom had eased his conscience and guilt some, but mainly, without knowing it, the call brought my son down from his anger by forcing him into a time-out from the crisis on the playground.

Although he hadn't been much of a follower of Sesame Street, my son liked Bert and Ernie, probably because they reminded him of the love-hate relationship he had with his own younger brother. In both cases, constant bickering provoked daily challenges to the ability of each pair of guys to co-exist. Of course, puppets are great at reading scripts, but in real life, there are no scripts, and children are not very skilled in controlling strong feelings and reactions. It is usually after the fact that they learn the consequences for impulsive behavior.

One of the best lessons Ernie taught my children was to look at making choices from the consequences-end of the decision-making process. To see the end first and think about all the possible outcomes for making a particular decision before taking action is consciousness and conscience at work. As my 9 year old was able to imagine the logical consequences he could expect, both at home and at school, for choosing to willfully pound on his classmate, the smack-down suddenly lost its charm. He saw the best choice for the outcome he wanted, because he was able to think ahead and take control of his anger instead of furiously acting on it and losing all the privileges he enjoyed. In his mind, a temporary explosion and moment of victory wasn't worth the cost.

More violent crimes are committed in the United States by children and teenagers than ever before. Shooting an infant in a stroller, slashing a teacher to death at school, or dragging a couple from their car and nearly beating them to death, minor-aged children are exacting death sentences on society and each other with unprecedented ease. Due to the seriousness of their crimes, minor aged kids are more frequently being tried in adult courts instead of juvenile. What is frightening is how many violent, juvenile crimes are pre-meditated, well-planned and *consciously intentional.* Whether enacted by child or adult, *violence is crime against us all.* It negatively impacts our collective consciousness as well as our individual sense of well-being by destroying the basic structure of our society.

Boundaries between children and adults have become blurred, rendering fear and distrust across all age groups. By essentially eliminating any expectation of age-appropriate and responsible behavior, we have enabled a subset of culture that is without accountability. When little is expected, little is returned. What used to be called juvenile delinquency has escalated to adult felony among too many youth of America. Saturated with violence in games, movies, music, social media, school, at home and in their communities, millions of children have become accustomed to crime and death.

AMNESIA

An angry society shares many characteristics with Africanized (killer) honey bees. The consciousness of the hive is devoted to protection of the queen and the production of honey, with which they are normally peacefully engaged. But if the bees are disturbed by so much as a sound or movement, they swarm aggressively to defend the hive. They are an acutely agitated species of animal that has become overly defensive and offensive, attacking in large numbers without provocation and stinging relentlessly until a perceived threat is rendered no longer a threat. Africanized bees are the result of genetic engineering that accidentally produced a honey bee version of Frankenstein. Killer bees are violent, consummate survivors incapable of changing their own destiny as a dangerous species. They are deranged fanatics, doing whatever it takes to stay alive.

America is like an angry hive that is swarming terribly out of control. Over-stressed and anxious, we have lost sight of the nectar that is our existence: our families, homes, and happiness. Our environment has become unsafe and threatening in the sickening toxicity of mayhem, so we react with fear and uncertainty. We are a colony without peace, confused by the drug of our collective anger and searching for home without direction or leadership. We want the sweet honey so bad we can taste it, but we have lost our way in the frenzied bedlam. Exhausted and disoriented, our flight is impaired and our will has been weakened, but we remember the smell of the flower.

Across the fruited plain the rose still blooms, and the garden still flourishes, untainted and ready to harvest. Unlike the poor killer bee, accidentally condemned to a life of chaos through no fault of their own by human intervention and error, we are each the masters of our destinies. It is in our DNA to reclaim our souls on the eve of destruction as our ancestors have done before us. Each of us are the engineers who will collaborate in the making of our future together. Lessons from history show us how, if we are willing to learn, and make teaching accurate history an important part of our children's education.

Roger Mudd, veteran journalist and reporter noted that with so many media sources, "Americans no longer get a concise, responsible account of current or past events". With no interest or stimulation for what was news in the past, the whole nation is sort of left on its own. Neal Justin of the Star Tribune, Minneapolis in an article "They Knew their ABC's, but Not their JFK" referred to studies indicating that people born after 1982 don't know about John F. Kennedy or the Cold War of his presidency.

In a survey by Forbes Magazine, Russian President Vladimir Putin, former leader of the Soviet Union and brutal spy agency, the KGB, is viewed as the world's most powerful leader today. Something has gone terribly wrong with the memory of the world. It sees the ex-leader of a violent communist regime that reigned terror and genocide on millions of people, and once threatened the existence of most of North and South America as the most powerful person in the world. We have failed to remember and have failed to teach this vital aspect of our country's history. At the 50th anniversary of President Kennedy's assassination, America is a country that has forgotten her lessons.

Americans today don't know anything about the Cold War, or the psychological terrorism that the threat of nuclear war caused in our country and to the entire world, according to Larry May, Professor Emeritus at the University of Minnesota. President Kennedy's assassination was "when our country began losing faith in the government. The uncomfortable connection would explain the amnesia", the desire of the nation to forget such a devastating era and tragedy in America. But, he continues, "that discomfort is exactly why we need to focus on such vital facts in our history". It is also when America fully awakened to violence.

"Teaching nuance and mood" is important to understanding history, says Kathrine Hayes, assistant professor of anthropology at the University of Minnesota, specializing in historical memory. "History can inform our current problems. We often appear to be repeating our mistakes because we don't remember what happened in the past." Clearly, the current high degree of amnesia in America has served us poorly. In not remembering our past, our foundational principles and our greatness as a people and nation, we have forfeited our progress and failed our children. Repeating history is the hallmark of insanity and tells us we are asleep on our watch. While sleeping, the serpent awakens and draws on our weaknesses only to keep stunning us with another act of violence.

Acts of violence of any kind do not develop in isolation. Somebody knows something. Terrorism requires a mentality of violence in order to flourish. It takes organized, systematic collaboration in order to make it happen, because it is a co-creation between like minds. According to a CNN report by Erin Burnett, global acts of terrorism are on the rise. There were 69% more in 2012 than 2011 with 89% more deaths; and those numbers are expected to continue to rise.

It is important to understand the relationship between terrorism and domestic violence. The common denominator is denial. Denial that there is a relationship, denial that we are individually and collectively part of it, and denial that we can do anything to stop it from escalating and destroying our lives. If we are drugged up, dummied down, apathetic and more concerned about hurting someone's feelings and political correctness than taking back our moral compass as a nation, we will not defeat our demons.

BACK IN THE SADDLE

If you get bucked off a horse, you'd best get right back on. Eating dust with a snake rattling at your toes isn't a good place to be, and a spooked horse won't wait around forever. It's a long walk back to the barn. America has fallen out of the saddle, and her symbolic horse is out of control. It's time to grab the reins and jump back on before the horse is gone.

At one of the worst times in our history, President Abraham Lincoln delivered a brief, simply crafted speech on a frigid battlefield at Gettysburg, Pennsylvania. It marked a turning point in the *Civil War* that decimated the nation. For the grief-stricken hearts of a disunited people, it was a blessing that would raise us up from despair. Fewer than three minutes long, the Gettysburg Address would inspire America to once again embrace the national ideals of freedom, liberty and justice on which our country was founded. Lincoln spoke of a new freedom, and his message would herald the resurrection of the Union of the United States of America.

The year 1783 marked the end of the Revolutionary War. It was America's triumph in the long battle for independence from England. Each terrible war demonstrated our indelible spirit as our new nation struggled into existence, and fought to retain her sovereignty. With faith, honor, allegiance and the "can do" spirit she was created in, America became the greatest country in the world. But, like the famous scene in Star Wars where the trash compactor is about to squeeze the life out of *Han Solo, Luke Skywalker, Princess Leia* and *Chewy,* America now finds herself stuck in the middle of a dumpster full of trash and serpents. We are in another war. The walls of deterioration are closing in. Societal violence has brought us once again to the threshold of a new beginning.

Intelligence is described on three levels: as *crystalized intelligence,* which is all the knowledge and information acquired over a lifetime, *emotional intelligence,* and *creative intelligence.* Humans have the ability to reinvent themselves by tapping into these three areas of creativity, according to Mark Walton, author of *Boundless Potential.*[1] By moving away from the "despair" model to the "hope" model of learning, we can build on our experiences, using choice and opportunity to improve our intelligence. But such a move requires the ability to know the difference between despair and hope. It also requires desire to change.

Leaving despair for hope is a wonderful path to follow in all areas of life, particularly in the learning process. *Overlapping memory* (memory that is linked with other memories), is the strongest type of learning. Memories that have relationship to each other have more meaning to us. As we understand the connection between them, they form a historical frame of reference. The lessons of history are especially valuable in learning how to grow from our mistakes. If we are smart, we won't make the same mistakes over and over. Instead, we can make better choices as a result of those mistakes. Because history links us to both the past and the future, learning from history is a very intelligent way to live; especially when it involves violence.

Milton Schwebel (1914-2013), distinguished professor, author, psychologist, and dean who served in the United States Army in WWII, was the founder of *Peace and Conflict: The Journal of Peace Psychology.* His obituary notes his fervently held belief that human beings possess the power to advance their intelligence. Humans, he asserted, can change their lives and circumstances, and achieve "peaceful solutions to conflict."[2] The key word quoted from Schwebel is "possess". Some people who possess this power will choose to change their lives and move their intellect into the future, he believed. But some will not. To *possess* is where the potential lies. Failure to utilize that potential is the problem. Un-used potential is wasted energy that could help make peace a greater possibility.

We may possess the power to advance our intellect, but we can't force anyone to move on it. All the potential and intelligence in the world is useless unless it is acted upon. It is important to use our intelligence to recognize the best path of action and change the direction our culture is headed in. To be vigilant, informed, aware and prepared doesn't deny that peace and peaceful solutions are possible. It means that every good general has Plan B. Not everyone is going to be on the good-guys team. The effort to create peace is advanced in good conscience and thwarted by evil. There will have to be more of us and less of them in order to succeed.

Galileo looked at stars and saw a great beyond. Far from the experience of his own life and eyes, he imagined eternity. In its radiant splendor, the astronomer envisioned an infinite universe. So he constructed a twenty-powered instrument and turned it toward the heavens and gazed into infinity. Marie Curie was a physicist who looked at atoms and saw unlimited energy. She believed in the possibility of seeing through matter by harnessing that energy. Her research with radioactive substances led to the use of radium to alleviate suffering, and the development of the X-ray. If we can dream, we can discover. Gandhi, Martin Luther King, and the Dalai Lama all dreamed of peace. Intelligence is in our genes. It's our job to wake up from the dream and take action to reduce the violence in our culture.

The highly-respected and now retired pediatric neurosurgeon, Ben Carson, M. D., enlists our hope and faith when he confers this notion: *One more educated disadvantaged or dropped-out child is one less person to fear or protect yourself and your family from; one less person to support through entitlements, and one less person for taxpayers to pay to incarcerate in the penal system. And that one child may have the ability to invent, create, or discover something beneficial to all of mankind.*[3]

Brain mapping, brain plasticity, super-brains and magnetic imaging show us how science sees our minds, and can reveal our thoughts, feelings and behaviors. Technology can even project who may become a criminal, an addict, or a killer. But nothing can see or predict the greatness of the spirit, or the wonder of the will when it is called upon to perform great feats in the face of adversity.

In his book, *The God particle: If the Universe is the Answer, What is the Question?"* Scientist Leon Lederman explains *"String Theory, or the theory of everything,"* as the standard model of particle physics.[4] The particle is believed to be the missing link, the key to the structure of the universe. The *Higgs bosons*, or: *the God particle*, as he called it, was named after Peter Higgs, who had earlier predicted its existence. If the theory is correct, then the entire world is made of 'strings'. The ties that bind us may be moving, shaking, and vibrating threads of continuous energy-*our universal intelligence.*

Higgs bosons were created 13 billion years ago, and with their discovery, we are now able to verify the elegant simplicity of our existence. Basic science reveals to us our fundamental capacity to become weak or strong, positive or negative, depending on which force attracts the most from its surrounding energy. Using this notion, we are all strings of the powerful particles of an endless universe which joins the strong with the weak to empower the most dominant mass.

The obvious is brilliantly clear. As interactive, shivering pieces of the whole of nature, intelligent and choreographed action is natural to our species. With conscience, discernment and intention, it is possible for humans to activate the strongest 'bosons' of our origins to create meaningful, purpose-driven lives. We need only become those particles magnetically attractive to the larger, stronger clusters of bosons to manifest our potential. It is in our *strings* to build on nature to organize a good, orderly direction for humanity. By focusing on our strengths, instead of our weaknesses, we are gifted with the power of the universe to change our world.

In his 1917 book of poetry, *Out Where the West Begins*, cowboy poet Arthur Chapman immortalized the kinder ways of a Western life.[5] His gentle verses speak of handshakes and smiles, and friendships that are truer. Of home, where the skies are bluer, and nature and bounty and song are alive, and hearts are freer of despair and aching. Of a place *where there is more of giving and less of buying,* and the sun shines brighter and the snow falls whiter….This is the place *where the West begins,* he mused. The poet's work embraces those ties that bind us and make our lives worth living. Chapman spoke affectionately of the way it was in a simpler time and place. It was where the buffalo still roamed, '*the deer and antelope played, and the skies were not cloudy all day'.* It is a memory we have not forgotten.

HEROES AND ORDINARY PEOPLE

America hungers for heroes almost as much as it does for ghoulish shows like Zombie Apocalypse and the Walking Dead. Comic Book Superheroes like Batman, Superman, and Wonder Woman have made a comeback. The heroes appeal to all ages and bring conviction and integrity back to life in our lives. Their tenacious feats of courage and devotion to good while overcoming evil show us the best in ourselves, and what we can be. In the Iron Man trilogy, we can believe that there are courageous among us, and that we ourselves are capable of becoming *Iron Patriots* too.

Marvel Superheroes were created on the fear of the Cold War in the 1930's and 1940's. The Hulk looked like he did because he had been inundated by gamma rays. He was radioactive, but overcame his problems on the strength of his character. Spider-man was a problematic teenager with no money and a lot of troubles in his life who suddenly changes when his uncle dies, and he takes responsibility for his death. The message of his character: "with great power comes great responsibility", is as important today as it was then.

Spider-man became the most famous of all comic book heroes because he was so real and so like *us.* Superheroes were ordinary citizens who became heroes because they possessed and *utilized* their extraordinary or superhuman abilities and skills. To have God-like powers and attributes is to bear the honor and virtue of all mankind.

They were characters with complex personalities who fought never-ending battles to protect and save America. It is our turn to be the super-heroes of our time and dedicate ourselves to the great particle in us all.

The popular television series, Duck Dynasty, experienced a meteoric rise to success. It is an example of the strong desire of grass-roots America to return to family values and traditions. Family members attribute the program's popularity to their conscious effort to retain the deeply rooted values they were raised with. The actors were born poor. Gratitude and a strong faith were the foundations of their humble lives before the series, and are the values they live by today. They are down-home people doing straight-forward, real life, and their audience loves them.

A sign in the halls of the Mendota Juvenile Detention facility in California encourages us all to our limitless potential: *"The expert in anything was once a beginner."* America is a unique, young country built by beginners. Experience and growing pains have taught us our expert-beginner can solve any problem. An example of the expert at work is a small town fighting to take back its freedom from violence. Nogales, Arizona, is a picturesque, hilly border town along the U.S. Mexico international border. It sits directly across the line from Nogales, Sonora, Mexico, its sister city. They sit in one of the most dangerous corridors of violence in America. Arizona is under the protection of the Tucson Sector of the United States Border Patrol. The Sector extends from the New Mexico State line to Yuma County. It is the busiest Sector in the country as apprehension of illegals and drugs, especially in Nogales, continues to escalate.

Daily violence on the Mexico side spills over the border with a vengeance. Fear and distrust hang like a shadow over the historic town. It sets a tone of unease and casts enormous stress on the people of the community. Domestic violence soared in the midst of crime that blanketed the area. So they came up with an ingenious and successful plan to help stop it. In a strong family culture like rural Nogales, Arizona, crimes of violence too often go unreported;

especially domestic violence. With money confiscated from organized crime, one police squad car has been painted *purple*. It is a passionate color for an emotionally-charged problem. The unusual car is a dramatic effort to break the silence of fear, and spread awareness against domestic violence. A large, easy to read phone number to call for help is painted white. The car, which is used for regular patrol duty, bears an important slogan:

Recognize it. Report it. Prevent it.

Puzzle pieces stenciled in white against the purple background represent how domestic violence tears families apart. Nogales created an awareness campaign to help people put the pieces and their families back together again. In the last year, domestic violence in the community decreased 15%, according to law enforcement. With ingenuity, courage and community support, they got it right. Nogales moved from a city in fear to a city of strength. They have taken back their freedom. The simple slogan on the car says it all.

When pterodactyls winged their way over a lush horizon, a hunter died and was frozen into the ice, and dogs became man's best friend, life was simple. Unlike dinosaurs, humans prevailed and emerged the victor over extinction. But in the process, our enlarging brains confounded the nature of things. Today we are co-inhabitants of a complex, unsafe world of our own making. Because we are hard-wired with the intelligence of the ages, we can break it all down and reclaim our sanity. What is required is the will of the ages to string it all back together again. Our culture is careening out of control. We are a nation unhinged by the madness claiming to be progress. Take up the reins, America, and bring the ponies home. It's time, once more, to live for that new birth of freedom Lincoln spoke of 150 years ago. There is a time for every season, and our season of rebuilding is now.

"ETERNAL VIGILANCE IS THE PRICE OF LIBERTY"

Aleut Memorial Headstone

Aleutian Pribilof Islands, Alaska

1981

NOTES

Chapter 1

1. Freud, Sigmund (1938). *The Basic Writings of Sigmund Freud.* New York, N.Y.: Modern Library, Random House, Inc.

2. Stout, Martha (2005). *The Sociopath Next Door: The Ruthless Versus the Rest of Us.* New York, N.Y.: Crown Publishing.

3. Montaldo, Charles: About.comcrime/Punishment.crime.about. com//: what is Stockholm syndrome? A strategy of survival.

4. Johnson Lewis, Jone: About.com Women's History. Rule of thumb and wife-beating – mostly a myth, another myth of women's history.

5. Dutton, Kevin (2013). *The Wisdom of Psychopaths: What Saints, Spies, and Serial Killers can Teach Us About Success.* New York, N.Y.: Farrar, Straus and Giroux.

Chapter 2

1. Von Goethe, Johanne Wolfgang (1828-1829). *Faust. The First Part of the Tragedy.* Germany. (1962) New York, N.Y.: Knopf Doubleday Publishing Group.

2. ! VIVEN! [http:www.fundacion'viven.org]. EAndes Accident Officialwebsite.

3. Rosenblatt, Carolyn: Forbes www.forbes.com// nurse – refuses to give Nurse Refuses to Give CPR, **Senior Dies**: Ethical Problem or Legal Issue? [March 3, 2013 @2:33 AM].

4. LaMance, Ken: LegalMatchLawLibrary [www.legalmatch.com/law/rape shield-law] *what are Rape Shield Laws?* : [June 10, 2012].

5. *SAHMSA* NEWS: Report Tracks America's Behavioral Health. beta.samhsa.gov//behavioral _health_barometer (Spring 2014) Volume 22, Number 2.

Chapter 3

1. **Cuban Missile Crisis** – John F. Kennedy Library and Museum http//: www.jfklibrary.org>JFD>JFK in History, **Cuban Missile Crisis**, 29 October 1962.

2. [en.wikipedia.org//The_Lord_of_the_Rings] Tolkien, J.R.R.: The **Lord_of_the_Rings: The Fellowship of the Rings.** Wikipedia, thefreeencyclopedia-1978 Film. (Last modified April 11, 2014).

3. By Mayo Clinic Staff: **Post-traumatic stress disorder** (PTSD**) Definition** – Diseases and Conditions [www.mayoclinic.org/post-traumatic-stress-disorder] April8, 2011.

4. Kuebler-Ross, M.D., Elizabeth (1970). *On Death and Dying.* New York, N.Y.: Macmillan.

5. A&E Television Networks, LLC the Holocaust – World War II - History.com [www.history.com/topics/ the holocaust [2014].

6. Spindler, Konrad (1996). *The Man in the Ice: The discovery of a 5,000–year-old Body Reveals the Secrets of the Stone Age.* Canada: Doubleday.

Chapter 4

1. Interview of German Minister of the Interior, Thomas de Maiziere,

2. Conducted by Joerg Schindler, Alfred Weinzierl and Peter Mueller **SPIEGEL** ONLINE - INTERNATIONAL: [www.spiegel. de > English Site > world, 'Us Operating Without and Kind of Boundaries', [April 9, 2014].

3. http://plato.stanford.edu/arhives/fall2009/entries/chaos/ Resmovits. Bishop, Robert, EdwardN.Zalta (ed.): "Chaos", *The Stanford Encyclopedia of Philosophy* (fall 2009edition).

Chapter 5

1. Press Office: [https://www.ed.gov/expansive –survey] ED.gov, U.S. Department of Education, Expansive survey of America's Public Schools Reveals Troubling Racial disparities: Lack of Access to Pre-School, Greater Suspensions Cited.

2. http://www.fbi.gov/ucr/cius2006/data/table_43.html; FBI Uniform Crime Reports, http://www.fbi.gov/ucr/ucr.htm. U.S. Government Arrest data by Race

3. Resmovits, Joy: [http://m.huffpost.com/us/entry/4374075/] Huffington Post. "U.S. Test Scores Remain Stagnant While Other Countries See Rapid Rise: [December 3, 2013, 05:00 AM ET].

4. Davis, Jack E.: Civil Rights Movement: https://www.scholastic. com//civil-rights-movement. An Overview l Scholastic.

5. Ander, Steve, and Swift, Art: "See Something, Say Something" Unfamiliar to Most, Gallop Politics, https://gallop.com/poll//see something-say-something: [December 23, 2013].

Chapter 6

1. http://ritualabuse.us/ritualabuse/studies/satani-ritual-abuse-evidence-with-information-on-the-mcmartin-preschool-case/; http://ritualabuse.us/ritualabuse/articles/survivorship-webinar-thee-aftereffects-of-extreme-child-abuse-and-the-resiliency-of-the-human-spirit/. List of Ritual Abuse and Satanic Ritual Abuse References:

2. www.crmi.om.au/images/files/Security_Solutions- TERRORISM AND **PREDICTIVE PROFILING** – CRMI, Complete Risk.

3. Brick, Michael: NY Times [www.nytimes.com/2010/, *Man Crashes Plane into Texas I.R.S. Office,* (published February 18, 2010).

4. Tom Cohen, Tom, Cratty, Carol, Frieden, Terry, and Silberleib, Alan, CNN Congressional Producer: no criminal prosecution of **Holder** for **contempt** - **CNN**.com [www.cnn.com/2012/holdercontempt, **Washington (CNN),** updated 9:23 AM EDT AM July 6, 2012.

5. **FAQonDomesticViolence: New Mexico** Coalition against **Domestic Violence** http://www.nmcadv.org ncdsv.org/images/DV_FAQs.pdf.

6. Kessler, Robert: NEWS MAX Independent American: [Monday 23 March 2009, 08:43 AM]. [www.newsmax.com/Napolitano.../3289 & 39 Man-Caused Disasters. **'MAN-CAUSED DISASTERS'** New Term for Terrorism]. Chapter 7.

7. Homer, The Internet Classics Archive l **The Odyssey**, translated by Samuel Butler, classics.mit.edu/Homer/**odyssey**.html, (800 B.C.E.).

8. Campbell, Joseph (1949). *The Hero with a Thousand Faces.* Novato, California: New World Library.

9. Guariglia, Matthew: Aaron Hernandez a Bloods Gang Member? [Tattoos - The Signs Are There [www.heavy.com/news/2013/06... hernandez-blood-gang-murder...aaron-hernandez] Published: 4:29pm EDT, June 27, 2013 l Updated: 9:31 am EDT, June 28, 2013.

10. [www.mylifetime.com/...house-of-Versace] *House of Versace* – Watch Lifetime Movies Online –myLifetime.com (2013).

11. Daily News: Trayvon Inc.: [www.nydailynews.com/...Trayvon-florida-teens] Florida teen's case turns into a brand with trademarked slogans, merchandise sales, [28 March, 2012, 06:22 PM].

12. Pearson, Michael & Mattingly, David: CNN [www.cnn.com/... florida-Zimmerman-defense. Guns, drugs, in new Trayvon Martin shooting evidence] updated 1:21 PM EDT 05.26.13h.

13. Shapiro, Ben (2013). *Bullies: How the Left's Culture of Fear and Intimidation Silences America.* New York, N.Y.: Simon and Schuster.

14. Meloy, J. Reid, (2000). *Violence Risk and Threat Assessment: A Practical Guide for Mental Health and Criminal Justice Professionals.* Orange County, California: Specialized Training Services.

15. Kearny, Laila: Reuters (www.reuters.com/../us-usa-crime) Smartphone Smartphone users oblivious to **gunman** who killed student on **train**: [Oct. 9, 2013].

Chapter 8

1. www.cdmc.ucla.edu/.../CDMC (PDF) **I Want My Fame TV: UCLA study finds that tweens receive a clear message from their favorite TV shows: Fame is the most important value**. Press release: [June 2011].

2. Eaton, Kristi: IOL News [www.iol.co.za/.../teenagers-charged-after Teenagers charged after jogger's death – World News l IOL News {August 21, 2013].

3. English,Greatist, Nick: USA Today News [www.usatoday.com/... internet-most-powerful-emotion] Anger is the Internet's most powerful emotion [September 24, 2013]

4. Gackenbach, Jayne, (2011*). Psychology and the Internet: Intrapersonal, Interpersonal, and Transpersonal Implications.* London, England: Academic Press.

5. Nahai, Natalie: Psychology Today [www.psychologytoday. com/.../angry-why-] Angry? Why **Rant Sites** May Do You More Harm Than Good [March 17, 2013, 6:12 am]

Back in the Saddle

1. Walton, Mark (2012). *Transform Your Brain, Unleash Your Talents, and Reinvent Your Work in Midlife and Beyond.* New York, N.Y.: McGraw-Hill Education.

2. Schwebel, Milton: [azstarnet.com/.../obituaries/Milton-Schwebel...Arizona Daily Star] (Tucson).

3. Carson, Benjamin S., (2014). *One Nation: What We Can All Do to Save America's Future.* USA: Penguin Group.

4. Klimas, Liz: [www.theblaze.com/.../the-god-particle-explained]. 'God Particle' Explained in Two Minutes by the Man Who Discovered It]: The Blaze [Feb 18 2014 7:00pm].

5. Chapman, Arthur (1917). *Out Where the West Begins: And Other Western Verses.* Boston: Houghton Mifflin.